MAKE
TODAY
COUNT

Also by John C. Maxwell:

RUNNING WITH THE GIANTS

TODAY MATTERS

THINKING FOR A CHANGE

ETHICS 101

MAKE
TODAY
COUNT

THE SECRET OF YOUR SUCCESS
IS DETERMINED BY YOUR DAILY AGENDA

JOHN C. MAXWELL

**CENTER
STREET®**

New York   Boston   Nashville

Scriptures noted NRSV are taken from THE NEW REVISED STANDARD
VERSION of the Bible. Copyright © 1989 by the Division of Christian
Education of the National Council of The Churches of Christ in the U.S.A.
All rights reserved.

Scriptures noted NIV are taken from the HOLY BIBLE: NEW
INTERNATIONAL VERSION®. Copyright © 1973, 1978, 1984 by
International Bible Society. Used by permission of Zondervan Publishing
House. All rights reserved.

Center Street
Hachette Book Group
1290 Avenue of the Americas
New York, NY 10104

www.centerstreet.com

Center Street is a division of Hachette Book Group, Inc. The Center Street
name and logo are trademarks of Hachette Book Group, Inc.

The publisher is not responsible for websites (or their content)
that are not owned by the publisher.

Printed in the United States of America
Originally published as *Today Matters* by Warner Faith

First Center Street Edition: June 2008
28 27 26 25 24 23 22 21 20

ISBN 978-1-59995-081-5

Book design by Charles Sutherland

CONTENTS

ACKNOWLEDGMENTS

I'd like to say thank you to:

Margaret Maxwell, who makes every day of my life great;

Charlie Wetzel, my writer;

Stephanie Wetzel, who proofs and edits every manuscript page;

and Linda Eggers, my assistant.

INTRODUCTION

Make Today a Masterpiece

How would you describe your life? Are you achieving what you desire? Are you accomplishing the things that are important to you? Do you consider yourself a success? How do your prospects look for the future?

If I could come to your house and spend just one day with you, I would be able to tell whether or not you will be successful. You could pick the day. If I got up with you in the morning and went through the day with you, watching you for twenty-four hours, I could tell in what direction your life is headed.

When I tell this to people at conferences, there's always a strong reaction. Some people are surprised. Some get defensive because they think I would be making a snap judgment about them. A few get ticked off because they think my claim sounds arrogant. Others are simply intrigued and desire to know why I make such a statement.

The answer lies in the fact that the secret of your success is determined by your daily agenda. If you make a few key decisions and then manage them well in your daily agenda, you will succeed.

You will never change your life until you change something you do daily. You see, success doesn't just suddenly occur one day in someone's life. For that matter, neither does failure. Each is a process. Every day of your life is merely preparation for the next. What you become is the result of what you do today. In other words . . . **You are preparing for something.** The way you live your life today is preparing you for your tomorrow. The question is, What are you preparing for? Are you grooming yourself for success or failure? As my father used to tell me when I was growing up, "You can pay now and play later, or you can play now and pay later. But either way, you are going to pay." The idea was that you can play and take it easy and do what you want today, but if you do, your life will be harder later. However, if you work hard now, on the front end, then you will reap rewards in the future.

THE MAKINGS OF A MASTERPIECE

You can make every day of your life a masterpiece. Isn't that idea appealing? The question is, How? What does it take? I believe there are two ingredients necessary to make every day a masterpiece: decisions and discipline. They are like two sides of the same coin; you could call them "goal setting" and "goal getting." And they can't be separated because one is worthless without the other. I say that because . . .

Good Decisions – Daily Discipline =
A Plan without a Payoff

Daily Discipline – Good Decisions =
Regimentation without Reward

Good Decisions + Daily Discipline =
A Masterpiece of Potential

Time is an equal opportunity employer, but how we treat time is not equal. Time is like a block of marble. Give a block of marble to an average person, and you end up with . . . a block of marble. But put it in the hands of a master sculptor, and watch what happens! The sculptor looks at it with an artist's eye. First, he makes decisions about what it will be. Then he practices the disciplines of his craft until he has transformed lifeless stone into a masterpiece. I believe you and I can become like the sculptor. We can learn to become master craftsmen, not of stone but of our lives.

GOOD DECISIONS TODAY WILL GIVE YOU A BETTER TOMORROW

It seems obvious that good decisions help to create a better tomorrow, yet many people don't appear to connect their lack of success to their poor decision making. Some people make choices, then experience negative consequences, yet wonder why they can't seem to get ahead in life. They never figure it out. Others know their choices may not be good for them, but they make them anyway.

Such is the case with the alcoholic who keeps drinking excessively or the person who engages in one abusive relationship after another.

Nobody says that good decisions are always simple, but they are necessary for success. Theodore Hesburgh, former president of Notre Dame University, admonished:

> You don't make decisions because they're EASY;
> You don't make decisions because they're CHEAP;
> You don't make decisions because they're POPULAR;
> You make decisions because they're RIGHT.

You begin to build a better life by determining to make good decisions, but that alone is not enough. You need to know what decisions to make. I've given the subject a lot of thought, talked to many successful people, and narrowed down the list of critical areas for success to twelve. I call them the "Daily Dozen":

1. **Attitude:** Choose and display the right attitude daily.
2. **Priorities:** Determine and act on important priorities daily.
3. **Health:** Know and follow healthy guidelines daily.
4. **Family:** Communicate with and care for my family daily.
5. **Thinking:** Practice and develop good thinking daily.

6. **Commitment:** Make and keep proper commitments daily.
7. **Finances:** Make and properly manage dollars daily.
8. **Faith:** Deepen and live out my faith daily.
9. **Relationships:** Initiate and invest in solid relationships daily.
10. **Generosity:** Plan for and model generosity daily.
11. **Values:** Embrace and practice good values daily.
12. **Growth:** Seek and experience improvements daily.

If you settle these twelve issues by making the right decision in each area and then work to manage those decisions daily, you can be successful.

MAKE
TODAY
COUNT

1

ATTITUDE

I discovered the importance of attitude in 1964 when I was seventeen years old. My high school basketball coach, Don Neff, took me aside at the beginning of my senior season and told me that he wanted me to be captain of the team. I was excited, but I was also a little surprised, because I knew that my teammate John Thomas was a better player than I was. But then Coach Neff said something that explained it. "John," he said, "you have the best attitude on the team, and it influences the other players."

Just a few weeks later, I was named "Citizen of the Month" at my school. Why? Once again, it was because of my attitude. My teachers said they loved my attitude. Then it sank in. My attitude was making a difference in my life. And it was making an impact on the people around me. That's when I made my attitude decision: *I am going to keep a positive attitude and use it to influence others.*

Many people in this world mistakenly believe their attitude is set. It has become such a habit for them that they believe it can't be changed. They see it as one of the "cards" of life they've been dealt, such as height or a history of cancer in the family. But that's not true.

MAKING THE DECISION TO CHOOSE AND DISPLAY THE RIGHT ATTITUDE DAILY

Your attitude is a choice. If you desire to make your day a masterpiece, then you need to have a great attitude. If it's not good now, you need to change it. Make the decision. Here's how:

Take Responsibility for Your Attitude

After my wife, Margaret, and I had been married for four or five years, we went to a conference for pastors where I had been asked to be one of the speakers. Margaret also agreed to do a breakout session for spouses. Speaking is not a passion for her as it is for me. She does a good job, but she doesn't really enjoy it that much. I wanted to support her, so I attended her session. During the Q and A time, a woman stood up and asked, "Does John make you happy?"

I have to say, I was really looking forward to hearing Margaret's answer. I'm an attentive husband, and I love Margaret dearly. What kind of praise would she lavish on me?

"Does John make me happy?" she considered. "No, he doesn't." I looked to see where the closest exit was. "The first two or three years we were married," she continued, "I thought it was John's job to make me happy. But he didn't. He wasn't mean to me or anything. He's a good husband. But nobody can make another person happy. That was my job."

As a young newlywed in her early twenties, she figured out something some people never learn. Each of us must take responsibility for our own attitude. If you want today to be a good day, you need to take charge of the way you look at it.

Decide to Change Your Bad Attitude Areas

I've read the *Peanuts* comic strip for years, and I've always been a big fan. I recall one strip in which Lucy announces, "Boy, do I feel crabby."

Her little brother, Linus, always anxious to relieve tension at home, responds, "Maybe I can be of help. Why don't you just take my place here in front of the TV while I go and fix you a nice snack? Sometimes we all need a little pampering to help us feel better." Then Linus brings her a sandwich, a few chocolate chip cookies, and some milk.

"Now, is there anything else I can get you?" he asks. "Is there anything I haven't thought of?"

"Yes, there's one thing you haven't thought of," Lucy answers. And then she suddenly screams, "I don't want to feel better!"

For the many years the late Charles Schulz drew *Peanuts*, that always seemed to be one of Lucy's problems. She didn't want to change in the areas where she had a bad attitude—and she had a lot of them!

Many people are like her. I mentioned that there are things in your life you cannot choose, such as your parents, where you were born, or your race. But your attitude is something you can change. And just about everybody has at least a few areas in their thinking that could use some help. If you want to have a better day, then you need to go after those areas.

Think, Act, Talk, and Conduct Yourself Like the Person You Want to Become

If you've been to any kind of class reunion ten or more years after graduation, then you've probably been surprised by the transformation of one of your former classmates—the misfit who became a famous lawyer, the plain Jane who blossomed into a movie star, or the geek who founded a major corporation. How do such transformations occur? Those people changed how they thought of themselves. You saw them as they were (or how you thought they were). They saw themselves as they *could* be. Then they learned to act like and acquire the skills of the people they wanted to be. The transformation usually takes time; often it's barely noticeable to those who see them every day (just as parents don't see changes in babies the way others do). But to someone who hasn't seen them in ten, twenty, or thirty years, the transformation seems miraculous, like a butterfly from a caterpillar.

If you desire to change yourself, then start with your mind. Believe you can improve, that you can change into the person you desire to be. Ralph Waldo Emerson said, "What lies behind us and what lies before us are tiny matters compared to what lies within us." If your thinking changes, then everything else can follow.

Place a High Value on People

One of the secrets of maintaining a good attitude is valuing people. You can't dislike people and have a good attitude at the same time. Think about it: Have you ever met anyone who always treated people badly but had a positive attitude? Likewise, you cannot have a bad attitude and encourage others at the same time. Encouraging others means helping people, looking for the best in them, and trying to bring out their positive qualities. That process drives negative thoughts right out of your head.

Your interaction with others sets the tone of your day. It's like the music of your life. When your interaction with others is poor, it's like having to listen to cacophonous music. But when you place a high value on people and you treat them well, it's like listening to a sweet melody as you go through your day.

Develop a High Appreciation for Life

Have you ever known people who complain about everything? Their soup's too hot. Their bed's too cold. Their vacation's too short. Their pay's too low. You sit side by side with them at a magnificent banquet, and while you enjoy every morsel, they tell you what's wrong with each and every dish. Such people don't appreciate life no matter how good it gets.

A friend e-mailed to me the story of a very "together" and independent ninety-two-year-old lady who was moving into a nursing home. Since she was legally blind and her husband of seventy years had passed away, the move was her only option. She waited in the lobby of the facility for a long time before finally being told that her room was ready. As she was escorted down the corridor, her attendant described the room, down to the curtains hung on the windows.

"I love it," the elderly lady enthused.

"But you haven't even seen the room yet. Just wait," the attendant responded.

"That doesn't have anything to do with it," she replied. "Happiness is something you decide on ahead of time. Whether I like my room or not doesn't depend on how the furniture is arranged. It's how I arrange my mind."

Appreciation isn't a matter of taste or sophistication. It's a matter of perspective. John Wooden said, "Things turn out best for the people who make the best of the way things turn out." The place to start is with the little things. If you can learn to appreciate them and be grateful for them, you'll appreciate the big things as well as everything in between.

MANAGING THE DISCIPLINE OF ATTITUDE

If you want to benefit from the possibilities of a positive attitude, you need to do more than just make the decision to be positive. You also have to manage that decision. For me, in the area of attitude it means one thing: ***Every day I will make the adjustments necessary to keep my attitude right.*** If this is new territory for you, you may be wondering how to do it. Here are some guidelines to help you on your way:

Recognize That Your Attitude Needs Daily Adjustments

I've discovered that a person's attitude does not naturally or easily stay positive. For example, a lifelong attitude weakness I've had is my impatience with people. It was a problem even back when I was young. In school, when the teacher set aside a day to review before the final exam, I got dirty looks when I asked, "If we got it the first time, do we still have to come for the review?" And I still fight impatience. Every day I ask myself, "Have I been impatient with someone?" When I have, I apologize to the person. I've had to do that more times than I'd like to admit.

Like any discipline, your attitude will not take care of itself. That's why it needs to be attended to daily. The stronger your natural inclination to be pessimistic or critical, the more attention your attitude will need. Begin each day with an attitude check. And watch for red flags signaling that your attitude might be in trouble.

Find Something Positive in Everything

Not long ago I came across a prayer that I thought was wonderful. It said,

Dear Lord,
   So far today, I am doing all right. I have not gossiped, lost my temper, been greedy, grumpy, nasty, selfish, or self-indulgent. I have not whined, cursed, or eaten any chocolate.
   However, I am going to get out of bed in a few minutes, and I will need a lot more help after that. Amen.

It may not always be easy, but if you try hard enough, you can find something good, even in the midst of difficult situations. In *Laugh Again*, my friend Chuck Swindoll explains that when Mother Teresa was asked the requirements for people assisting in her work with the destitute in Calcutta, she cited two things: the desire to work hard and a joyful attitude. If someone could be expected to be joyful among the dying and the poorest of the poor, then certainly we can do the same in our situation.

Find Someone Positive in Every Situation

Nothing helps a person to remain positive like having an ally. The world is filled with negative people; in fact, they often flock together. But positive people are everywhere, too. You'll often find them soaring above the negative people—like eagles. When you do, seek them out. If you're having a hard time, get close and "draft" behind them the way racers do. If they're having difficulty, you be the one to go out front and make things easier. Two positive people are much better at fighting off the blues than someone going it alone.

Say Something Positive in Every Conversation

I've tried to make it a habit to include positive comments in every conversation with others. It starts with those closest to me. When my wife looks beautiful (which is *often*!) I tell her so. I compliment my children every time I see them. And I absolutely pour out praise every time I see my grandchildren. But I don't stop there. I sincerely compliment, praise, acknowledge, bolster, raise up, and reward people whenever I can. It's wonderful for me as well as for others. I highly recommend it, and I know you can learn to do it, too.

Remove Negative Words from Your Vocabulary

My father retired in his midseventies, but he has spent his entire life in public speaking. He came from a modest background, so he was always working hard to learn and grow. When I was a kid, he used to pay my brother, Larry, and me ten cents for every grammatical mistake we found him making when he was preaching. It was just one example of how he was constantly trying to improve himself. (I suspect he also did it so that we would learn more about grammar ourselves.)

You can do a similar kind of thing when it comes to your attitude. You—or someone you enlist—can be on the lookout for negative words in your vocabulary so that you can try to eliminate them. Here's a list to get you started:

Eliminate These Words	Say These Instead
I can't	I can
If only	I will
I don't think	I know
I don't have the time	I will make the time
Maybe	Absolutely
I'm afraid	I'm confident
I don't believe	I'm sure

If you continually look for and embrace the positive and eliminate the negative, you'll help yourself to begin thinking more positively every day.

Express Gratitude to Others Daily

Of all the virtues, gratitude seems to be the least expressed. How often do people go out of their way to thank you? How often do you receive a thank-you note when you give a gift? More important, how often do you extend your thanks to others? In our culture of plenty, we tend to take things for granted.

A few years ago, Oprah Winfrey encouraged her millions of TV viewers to keep a gratitude journal to help them appreciate life. Amy Vanderbilt, journalist and etiquette book author, said, "When we learn to give thanks, we are learning to concentrate not on the bad things, but on the good things in our lives." Thinking about the good things helps us to be grateful. Remaining grateful helps us to have a more positive attitude. And having a positive attitude prompts us to think about the good rather than the bad. It's a positive cycle that helps to fuel itself.

Your Attitude Decision Today

Where do you stand when it comes to your attitude today? Ask yourself these three questions:

1. Have I already made the decision to choose and display the right attitude daily?
2. If so, when did I make that decision?
3. What exactly did I decide?

Your Attitude Discipline Every Day

Based on the decision you made concerning attitude, what is the one discipline you must practice *today and every day* in order to be successful?

2

PRIORITIES

When I first graduated from college and began my career, I was not working according to my own agenda. Back in the 1960s when I studied for the ministry, the majority of my course work had prepared me to do counseling and administration. So when I began working in 1969, guess what I spent most of my time doing. That's right, counseling and administration. Nothing could have been further from my natural gifts—or my natural inclinations. Despite much hard work, I was neither fulfilled nor effective.

Because I wanted to improve myself and pick up skills I didn't learn in college, in 1971 I began working on a business degree. While reading for one of the courses, I came across a paragraph written about Italian economist Vilfredo Pareto. It contained information about prioritizing called the Pareto Principle. It said that by focusing your attention on the top 20 percent of all your priorities, you would get an 80 percent return on your effort. That was my eureka moment! That's when

I made this decision: *I will prioritize my life and give focus and energy to those things that give the highest return.*

I never looked at myself or my work in the same way again. I realized that I needed to focus 80 percent of my time, energy, and resources on my areas of strength, not on counseling and administration. Those activities were not bad things. They were just bad things for me. From the moment I made that decision, I have been a practitioner of the Pareto Principle, and I have taught it to others for thirty-three years. (If you want to read a more in-depth treatment of the Pareto Principle, read my book *Developing the Leader Within You*.)

Most of the time this has kept me focused and on track, although when I first began applying the principle, the results sometimes were not what I had intended. Margaret and I still laugh about the time she asked me to start helping her mow the lawn. "Margaret," I said, having just learned Pareto, "I don't want to waste time on something like that. I'm trying to stay focused. We can *pay* somebody to do that."

Margaret looked at me and replied, "Pay with what?" We worked it out, but it was a defining moment for us. From that time on, I have tried to focus on those things that are important and not get sidetracked.

MAKING THE DECISION TO DETERMINE AND ACT ON IMPORTANT PRIORITIES DAILY

If you want to change the way you look at yourself and what you do by making a decision concerning your priorities, then do the following:

Take Back Today

Have you ever noticed that the people who have nothing to do usually want to spend their time with you? Poet Carl Sandburg said, "Time is the most valuable coin in your life. You and you alone will determine how that coin will be spent. Be careful that you do not let other people spend it for you."

Your greatest possession is the twenty-four hours you have directly ahead of you. How will you spend it? Will you give in to pressure or focus on priorities? Will you allow pointless e-mails, unimportant tasks, telemarketers, interruptions, and other distractions to consume your day? Or will you take complete responsibility for how you spend your time, take control of the things you can, and make today yours? If you don't decide how your day will be spent, someone else will.

Ask Yourself Three Questions

No Daily Dozen issue has added more to my success than the principle of priorities. When I discovered that I needed to change my approach to my day and my career, I started by asking myself three critical questions:

1. **What is *required* of me?** Any realistic assessment of priorities in any area of life must start with a realistic assessment of what a person *must* do. For you to be a good spouse or parent, what is required of you? To satisfy your employer, what must you do? (If you lead others, then the question should be, What must

you personally do that cannot be delegated to anyone else?) When ordering priorities, always start with the requirement question and give it careful thought before moving on to the next question.

2. **What gives me the greatest *return*?** As you progress in your career, you begin to discover that some activities yield a much higher return for the effort than others do. (Anyone who hasn't discovered that probably *isn't* progressing in his career!) The next place to focus your attention is on those high-return activities.

3. **What gives me the greatest *reward*?** If you do only what you must and what is effective, you will be highly productive, but you may not be content. I think it's also important to consider what gives you personal satisfaction. However, I find that some people want to start with the *reward* question and go no further than that. No one can be successful who doesn't possess the discipline to take care of the first two areas before adding the third.

Philosopher William James said, "The art of being wise is the art of knowing what to overlook." If you bring your priorities into focus by answering those three questions, you will have a much better idea of what you should overlook.

Stay in Your Strength Zone

People don't pay for average. People don't go looking for a mediocre restaurant and middling movie when they go out at night. Employers don't award the contract to the salesman known as Mr. Average. Nobody says, "Let's give the contract to the company that will do a merely adequate job."

It was a great day in my church when I stopped counseling people and stopped getting bogged down in administrative details. But finding my strength zone took some time and exploration. If you don't already have a good handle on your strengths, then you may want to explore some of these suggestions. They're based on what I did to find mine:

- **Trial and error:** Nothing teaches you more than your successes and failures. Any time something seems to be all "trial," and you make a lot of mistakes, it's probably time to move on. But you've got to take the risk of failing to find your successes.
- **The counsel of others:** Asking others to evaluate your effectiveness is not always fun, but it is always helpful. Be sure to choose people who don't have an agenda—other than to help you.
- **Personality tests:** Evaluations, such as DISC, Florence Littauer's Personality Profile, and Myers-Briggs, can be very helpful. They will help to clarify some of your natural inclinations and help to reveal some strengths and weaknesses you aren't aware of.
- **Personal experience:** You really get a feel for how well you do something by doing it repeatedly. Just remember this: Experience isn't always the best teacher—evaluated experience is!

British prime minister William Gladstone said, "He is a wise man who wastes no energy on pursuits for which he is not fitted; and he is wiser still who from among the things he can do well, chooses and resolutely follows the best." The more you stay in your strength zone, the greater your productivity and the greater your ability to reach your potential.

MANAGING THE DISCIPLINE OF PRIORITIES

One of the things I noticed very quickly after making my priorities decision was that priorities shift very easily. For that reason they must be continually evaluated and guarded. My reminder to manage the discipline of priorities is this: *Every day I will live my life according to my priorities.* What does that mean? Five things:

1. Evaluate Priorities Daily

A man went to the Super Bowl and climbed to the top row in the end zone section of the stadium to reach his seat. After the game started, he spotted an empty seat on the fifty-yard line. After working his way down to it, he asked the man in the next seat, "Excuse me, but is anyone sitting here?"

"No," replied the man. "Actually, the seat belongs to me. I was supposed to come with my wife, but she died. This is the first Super Bowl we haven't been to together since we got married in 1967."

"That's very sad. But still, couldn't you find anyone else to take the seat—a relative or close friend?"

"No," replied the man, "they're all at the funeral."

Priorities don't stay put; you have to revisit them every day. Why? Because conditions continually change. So do methods of getting things done. Your values, once defined, are going to be steady. You will be able to rely on them. But how you carry them out needs to be flexible.

2. Plan Your Time Carefully

According to a survey taken by Day-Timers, Inc., only one-third of American workers plan their daily schedules. And only 9 percent follow through and complete what they planned. If you want to be effective, you must be able to make the transition to planning. I plan my calendar forty days at a time. But when I get ready to approach a day, I have the whole thing laid out. Hour by hour. It's a rare day that I get up in the morning wondering what I will be doing that day—even when on vacation.

3. Follow Your Plan

I don't mean to insult your intelligence by suggesting that you follow your plan, but it needs to be said. According to time management expert Alec Mackenzie, surveys show that most executives don't get to their most important tasks until midafternoon. Why? Most finished off low-priority tasks so that they could have a sense of accomplishment.[1]

German novelist Johann Wolfgang von Goethe said, "Things that matter most must never be at the mercy of things that matter least." If you prioritize your life and plan your day but don't follow through, your results will be the same as those of someone who didn't prioritize at all.

4. Delegate Whenever Possible

I've observed that most people fall into one of two categories when it comes to delegation: They're either clingers or dumpers. Clingers refuse to let go of anything they think is important—whether they are the best person to do it or not. Their goal is perfection. Dumpers are quick to get rid of tasks, yet give little thought to how successful their delegation efforts will be. Their goal is to get things off their desk.

How do you find the right standard for delegation? When is it right to hand something off, and when is it right to hold on to it? Here's the guideline I use: If someone else can do a task I'm doing 80 percent as well as I do, then I hand it off. That's pretty darned good. And if I do a good job of motivating, encouraging, and rewarding them, then they will only get better. I've handed off responsibilities using that standard, and after a while, the person who's taken on the job has gone on to do it much better than I could. When that happens, it's very rewarding.

Today I am surrounded by people on my team who do things much better than I can. They make up the difference in my weak areas, and they exceed my expectations in others. They lift me to a level higher than I could ever attain myself, and they allow me to live out my priorities. The advice of management expert Peter Drucker is good: "No executive has ever suffered because his subordinates were strong and effective."

5. Invest in the Right People Daily

There's one more area I want to address in the area of priorities, and that's the need to prioritize how we spend time with people. My friend Waylon Moore has observed that often "we spend priority time with problem people when we should be spending it with potential people." I think that's true.

How do you decide whom to spend time with? Certainly, you want to treat everyone with respect and try to have a good, positive relationship with everyone. But you should not spend time with everyone equally. Here's what I use to evaluate where to invest my time:

- Value to the team
- Natural ability
- Responsibility
- Timing
- Potential
- Mentoring fit

The time you spend with others can be a great investment. Choose whom you will invest in, and then add value to them on a consistent basis. You will never regret it.

Your Priorities Decision Today

Where do you stand when it comes to priorities today? Ask yourself these three questions:

1. Have I already made the decision to determine and act on important priorities daily?
2. If so, when did I make that decision?
3. What exactly did I decide?

Your Priorities Discipline Every Day

Based on the decision you made concerning priorities, what is the one discipline you must practice *today and every day* in order to be successful?

3

HEALTH

I need to begin this chapter by making a confession. Usually when people pick up a book, especially a book that contains advice, they expect the author to be an expert in every area he writes about. That is not the case with me when it comes to health.

For much of my life, I have dropped the ball in this area. It was really more a matter of neglect than anything else. I've always been as healthy as a horse. In thirty years of public speaking, first as a pastor and then as a conference and seminar leader, I have never missed an engagement due to illness. Not one! I just don't get sick, and I've always had lots of energy. Even when I had to burn the candle at both ends, I still had plenty of energy left over.

I have lived a very fast-paced life. For about ten years, I held down two demanding jobs. I led a church of more than three thousand people with a staff of over fifty and a budget of $5 million a year. At the same time, I led a leadership development organization that required me to travel to speak more than one hundred days a year.

Maintaining a lifestyle at that pace meant that I rarely exercised, I didn't eat well, and I was overweight. But I didn't worry. Every year I took a physical and received an excellent report from my doctor. So I simply took my health for granted.

All that changed for me on December 18, 1998. That was the night of the annual Christmas party for my employees and their spouses. At the end of the party, I didn't feel well. One of my employees gave me a good-bye hug and felt cold sweat on the back of my neck. Then suddenly I felt an excruciating pain in my chest that brought me to my knees. I had never experienced anything like it. As I lay on the floor awaiting the paramedics, it felt like an elephant was sitting on my chest. I was grateful that Margaret, our children, and many of my closest friends were there with me at the party, because I thought I wasn't going to make it.

When I got to the hospital, I was told I was having a serious heart attack. As I lay in the emergency room for the next few hours with doctors trying different treatments, none of which seemed to be working, my assistant, Linda Eggers, made a phone call. Six months earlier a cardiologist from Nashville named John Bright Cage had met me for lunch and shared his concern for my health. At the end of our conversation, he said that if I ever needed his help, I could call him, day or night, and he included his home phone number. So even though it was 2:00 A.M., Linda called him. Less than an hour later, in walked Dr. Jeff Marshall and some of his colleagues, announcing, "The A-team is here." Dr. Cage had called one of the finest cardiologists in Atlanta and asked him to help me.

In the wee hours of the morning, Dr. Marshall performed a procedure to remove a clot that had made its way into my heart. He saved my life. Afterward, he explained that he had used a new procedure that had only recently been developed. If I'd had my heart attack a year or two earlier, nothing could have been done. It would have killed me!

As I recovered from my heart attack in the hospital, I felt very fortunate to be alive. Cardiovascular diseases are the number-one cause of death in the United States and Europe.[2] But I didn't discover how blessed I was until Dr. Marshall told me that I had sustained no damage to my heart. That meant I had the potential to make a full recovery.

Dr. Marshall told me that men who survive an early heart attack (and learn from it) often live longer and healthier lives than those who never suffer a heart attack. The key to my future health would be whether I was willing to make the decision to change the way I lived and stick with it. So, at the age of fifty-one, I made this health decision: *I will take good care of myself by exercising and eating right.*

MAKING THE DECISION TO KNOW AND FOLLOW HEALTHY GUIDELINES DAILY

If you know the value of good health, yet you've had a hard time making the commitment to know and follow healthy guidelines, here are some suggestions to help you turn your attention to the subject and tackle it:

Have a Purpose Worth Living For

Nothing is better than perspective for helping a person want to do the right thing. When you have something to live for, not only does it make you desire a long life, but it also helps you to see the importance of the steps along the way. Seeing the big picture enables us to put up with little irritations.

It's hard to find motivation in the moment when there is no hope in the future. A sense of purpose helps a person to make a decision to change and then to follow through with the discipline required to make that change permanent. I found that to be true after my heart attack. A friend who spent a lot of time with me during my recovery saw me pass on desserts time after time—something that was not characteristic of me—and finally he asked, "Have you lost your craving for desserts?"

"No," I answered, "but my craving for life is greater."

Do Work You Enjoy

One of the greatest causes of debilitating stress in people's lives is doing jobs they don't enjoy. It's like comedienne Lily Tomlin said, "The problem with the rat race is that even if you win, you're still a rat." I believe two major frustrations contribute to that stress. The first is doing work you don't think is important. If you do work that you believe adds no value to yourself or to others, you quickly become demoralized. If you work in that state for a long time, it begins to wear you down. To remain healthy, your work must be in alignment with your values.

Another reason some people don't like their work is that they do jobs that keep them in an area of weakness. Nobody can do that long and succeed. For example, most people hate the thought of public speaking. How would you like to get up in front of an audience and speak to them every day? That's some people's number-one fear. But for me, that's my greatest joy. After speaking to people for six or seven hours at a conference, I'm not tired. I'm fired up! Speaking to an audience energizes me.

One of the ways you can tell you're working in an area of strength is that it actually gives you energy. Even if you are in the early stages of your career or are starting out on a new venture and you're not very good at something you're doing, you can still tell it's an area of strength by paying attention to how you respond to your failures. Mistakes that challenge you show your areas of strength. Mistakes that threaten you show your areas of weakness.

Find Your Pace

Mickey Mantle reportedly said, "If I had known I was going to live this long, I would have taken better care of myself." I think that statement could apply to many people as they age. Part of taking care of yourself includes finding and maintaining the pace that's right for you. If you take life more slowly than your energy level is capable of, you can become lazy. If you continually run at a pace faster than you are capable of, you can burn out. You need to find your balance.

As I mentioned previously, I've always been a high-energy person, and I always thought there was nothing I couldn't do. But in 1995, when I was forty-seven years old, I was so tired of leading my church and my own organization that I was worn out. I loved both, but doing them at the same time for over a decade was finally taking its toll on me.

One day I told Margaret, "I can't keep doing this. I've got to give up one or the other." Margaret had been advising me for years to cut back my busy schedule, but she was shocked by my statement.

"John," she said, "in all the years I've known you, that's the first time I've ever heard you say you are exhausted."

Even today, at age fifty-seven, I still have a tendency to take on too much and go at a faster pace than is really good for me. There are so many opportunities I want to pursue, books I want to write, and people I want to help. I'm constantly trying to strike a balance between my desire to maintain a healthy pace of life and my drive to accomplish all I can during my lifetime.

Accept Your Personal Worth

During the weeks and months after the terrorist attack on New York's World Trade Center, the song "God Bless America" regained popularity and was performed repeatedly at ball games and other events. The song was written by Irving Berlin, creator of innumerable popular and

Broadway hits such as "White Christmas," "Easter Parade," "Puttin' on the Ritz," and "There's No Business Like Show Business." Back when I lived in San Diego, I remember reading an interview with Berlin in the *Union Tribune* in which Don Freeman asked the songwriter whether there was a question he wished someone had asked him. Berlin replied, "Yes, there is one. 'What do you think of the many songs you've written that didn't become hits?' My reply would be that I *still* think they are wonderful!"

Berlin had a good sense of self-worth and confidence in his work, regardless of whether it was accepted by others. That's certainly not true of everyone. In fact, a poor or distorted self-image is the cause of many health-threatening conditions and activities, from drug use and alcoholism to eating disorders and obesity.

Psychologist Joyce Brothers says, "An individual's self-concept affects every aspect of human behavior. The ability to learn . . . the capacity to grow and change . . . the choice of friends, mates, and careers. It is no exaggeration to say that a strong positive self-image is the best possible preparation for success in life." If your self-image is driving you to do things that negatively affect your health, seek help.

Laugh

Physician Bernie S. Siegel wrote in *Peace, Love and Healing*, "I've done the research and I hate to tell you, but everybody dies—lovers, joggers, vegetarians and non-smokers. I'm telling you this so that some of you who jog at 5 a.m. and eat vegetables will occasionally sleep late and have an ice cream cone."[3]

We should never take life or ourselves too seriously. Each of us has idiosyncrasies that can cause us to despair or to laugh. For example, when it comes to anything related to tools or technology, I'm clueless. I'm not Mr. Handyman—I'm Mr. Hopeless. I don't let that bother me at all. If you can laugh at yourself loudly and often, you will find it liberating. There's no better way to prevent stress from becoming distress.

MANAGING THE DISCIPLINE OF HEALTH

For some people, the discipline of health appears to be easy. My friend Bill Hybels seems to manage it well. He eats well, runs regularly, and keeps his weight down. For years before I had my heart attack, he used to challenge me to take better care of myself. He used to joke to friends that while he was eating birdseed, I was eating steaks and rich desserts. He was right about it catching up with me. Although much of my problem was hereditary, my lifestyle made things worse.

After meeting with Dr. Marshall following my heart attack, I had a new discipline to manage: *Every day I will eat low-fat foods and exercise for at least thirty-five minutes.* He told me that 85 percent of all heart patients quit their healthy regimen within six months. Even though I had not succeeded in this area in my first fifty years, I was determined to succeed in it the rest of my life.

Margaret and I learned everything we could about heart issues, low-fat diets, and exercise. I became a model of discipline. And in May of 2001 when I visited Dr. Marshall, he congratulated me. "John," he said, "you're doing all the right things. You don't need to consider yourself a heart patient anymore."

I wish I had never heard those words. You see, I love food, and I possess a "foodaholic" bent. Because of the good news I received from Dr. Marshall, I gave myself permission to cheat on my diet once in a while—something I had not done even once in two and a half years. A few weeks later, Margaret and I went on vacation to London with some friends, and I ate food that I had not touched in all that time. I loved every bit of it, especially the fish and chips.

The problem was that I quit managing my life according to the decision I had made. I had relaxed my discipline. Once my commitment was less than 100 percent, I got into trouble. I need to exercise and stay on my diet every day. But I began to slide: from every day, to most days, to some days. I ignored my own teaching that *today matters*. Neglect enough todays, and you'll experience the "someday" you've wanted to avoid!

The good news is that I'm no longer "off the wagon." I'm recommitted to my daily discipline. The bad news is that I'm doing only 80 percent of what I was doing before. Dr. Marshall is trying to help me. He's a good doctor and a good friend, and he knows that sometimes the best medicine is a good kick in the butt. The area of health is still a battle, but it's one I'm determined to win. As I fight the good fight, I hope you'll join me by doing the following things daily:

Eat Right

It was Mark Twain who observed that "the only way to keep your health is to eat what you don't want, drink what you don't like, and do what you'd rather not." Twain was being cynical, but there's a lot of truth to what he said. If we could write our own rules for healthy eating, I think they would look something like this:

1. If no one sees you eat it, then it has no calories.
2. If you drink a diet soft drink with a candy bar, the calories are canceled out.
3. If you eat with a friend and you eat the same amount, the calories don't count for either of you.
4. Foods used for medicinal purposes never count: Examples include chocolate, brandy, and Sara Lee cheesecakes.
5. The secret of looking thinner is getting the people around you to gain weight.

The key to healthy eating is moderation and managing what you eat every day. Don't rely on crash diets. Don't worry about what you ate yesterday. Don't put off good eating until tomorrow. Just try to eat what's best for you in the moment. Focus on now.

If you're not sure how you're doing or what you should

(and shouldn't) be eating, get a physical. Your doctor will let you know how you're doing and how to change your diet.

Exercise

Most people I know either love exercise and do it excessively or they hate it and avoid it completely; yet consistent exercise is one of the keys to good health. Dr. Ralph S. Paffenberger, Jr., a research epidemiologist and physician at the University of California at Berkeley, performed pioneering studies that revealed the impact of exercise on health. Paffenberger states:

> We know that being physically fit is a way of protecting yourself against coronary heart disease, hypertension and stroke, plus adult-onset diabetes, obesity, osteoporosis, probably colon cancer and maybe other cancers, and probably clinical depression. Exercise has an enormous impact on the quality of life.[4]

Paffenberger, who ran 151 marathons, asserts that exercise is beneficial for people of all ages.

One of the tough things about exercising is that the immediate payoff seems so small. You weigh yourself after exercising. Nothing. You exercise the next day. Nothing. And the next day and the next. Still nothing. Then after the fifth day of exercise, maybe you see that you've lost half a pound. It's easy to get discouraged, especially when you don't see results most of the time. But your four days of discipline make the progress you see on the fifth day possible.

The key to success in this area is consistency. I exercise a minimum of five days a week by walking on a treadmill for at least thirty-five minutes a day. That's what my doctor has recommended. If you don't already practice the habit of daily exercise, then find a way to get started. It doesn't really matter what you do as long as you do it. Talk to your doctor. Hire a trainer. Do whatever it takes to begin a regimen that's right for you.

Handle Stress Effectively

A hundred years ago, most causes of illness were related to infectious disease. Today, they are related to stress. I once read a list of questions produced by the United Kingdom–based National Association for Mental Health to help a person gauge whether stress was becoming a problem. Here's what people were asked:

- Do minor problems and disappointments bother you more than they should?
- Are you finding it hard to get along with people (and them with you)?
- Have you found that you're not getting a kick out of things you used to enjoy?
- Do your anxieties haunt you?
- Are you afraid of situations or people that didn't bother you before?

- Have you become suspicious of people, even your friends?
- Do you ever feel that you are trapped?
- Do you feel inadequate?

If you answer yes to many of these questions, stress may be a problem for you. Everybody faces problems and feels pressure at times. Whether that pressure becomes stress depends on how you handle it. Here's how I handle issues to keep them from becoming stressful to me:

- **Family problems:** communication, unconditional love, time together
- **Limited options:** creative thinking, advice from others, tenacity
- **Staff productivity problems:** immediate confrontation with the person and addressing the issue
- **Staff leaders with bad attitudes:** removal

I've found that the worst thing I can do when it comes to any kind of potential pressure situation is to put off dealing with it. If you address problems with people as quickly as possible and don't let issues build up, you greatly reduce the chances of being stressed out.

Your Health Decision Today

Where do you stand when it comes to health today? Ask yourself these three questions:

1. Have I already made the decision to know and follow healthy guidelines daily?
2. If so, when did I make that decision?
3. What exactly did I decide?

Your Health Discipline Every Day

Based on the decision you made concerning health, what is the one discipline you must practice *today and every day* in order to be successful?

4

FAMILY

In 1986, when I was thirty-nine years old, I began to notice a terrible trend. The marriages of some of my colleagues, college buddies, and friends were falling apart and ending in divorce. That really got my attention because even some of the relationships that Margaret and I had considered to be strong had fallen by the wayside. We didn't think our relationship was in any kind of danger, but I also discovered that before their breakdowns, some of the couples had thought nothing like that could ever happen to them.

This all occurred about the same time my career was really taking off. I still wanted to be successful, but I didn't want to lose my family in the process. That prompted me to make one of my key life decisions, and I would do so by rewriting my definition of success. From that moment, *Success meant having those closest to me love and respect me the most.*

That decision put my wife, Margaret, and my children, Elizabeth and Joel, right in the middle of my definition of success. Success would be impossible if I achieved outwardly but failed to take my family with me on the journey. The applause of others would never replace the appreciation of my family. Respect from others meant little if I did not have the respect of my loved ones. I would make caring for and communicating with my family one of my life's priorities.

MAKING THE DECISION TO COMMUNICATE WITH AND CARE FOR MY FAMILY DAILY

I don't know where you stand with your family now; everyone's situation is unique. You may have a great family life. Or you may have made some serious mistakes from which you fear you will never recover. You may be single with no children, so that all you have is extended family. But I can tell you this: No matter what your situation is, you can benefit from the stability that comes from communicating with and caring for your family daily. Here's how to get started:

Determine Your Priorities

There's a Russian proverb that gives this advice:

> Before going to war—pray once.
> Before going to sea—pray twice.
> Before getting married—pray three times.

In other words, any time you're going to engage in a great (and potentially risky!) endeavor, give it serious consideration first. How else are you going to know where it ranks in priority in your life?

I began learning this lesson the hard way. In the space of one month in 1969, I graduated from college, got married to Margaret, and started my first job. As soon as we got back from our honeymoon, we moved to a new town and I started working. I was the senior pastor of a small country church, and I was determined to be successful. I threw myself into the job, giving it everything I had. And when I say everything, I mean *everything*. I worked all day at the church, and every evening I set appointments to meet with people in the community. I worked a six-day workweek, but I cheated by working on my day off, too. Meanwhile, Margaret worked a couple of jobs to keep us going financially because my salary was so low. The problem was that I was neglecting her and our marriage.

Margaret and I have known each other since high school, and we dated for six years before we got married, so we had a lot of history together, especially for a couple so young. Back then I believed our history was going to carry us through while I devoted myself to my career. But a marriage can't survive forever on leftovers. It needs to be fed continually, or it will eventually starve.

A lot of people are allowing their families to "starve." According to psychologist Ronald L. Klinger, president of the Center for Successful Fathering, parents spend 40 percent less time with children than parents of previous generations.[5] Families are breaking up at a terrible rate. Within five years, 20 percent of all first marriages end in divorce. Within ten years, that number rises to 33 percent.[6] More than a fourth of all families in the United States (28 percent in 2000) are headed by single parents.[7] And nearly three-fourths of children in single-parent families will experience poverty by the time they reach age eleven.[8] Every year, $20 billion to $30 billion in taxpayers' money goes to support children whose noncustodial parents neglect them financially.[9]

Building a solid family doesn't just happen on its own. You have to work at it. After I got the message that I was neglecting Margaret, I changed my approach to my career. I carved out time for her. I protected my day off. And we dedicated money in our budget to facilitate special times together. I still wanted to be successful, but not at the cost of my family! And I'm still working on making my family a priority. Anyone who neglects or abandons his family for fame, status, or financial gain isn't really successful.

Decide on Your Philosophy

Once you've determined to make your family a priority, you have to decide what you want your family to stand for. That should be based on your values. In the first decade of our marriage, Margaret and I decided on our personal philosophy of family. First, we tried to live it out as a couple. Then when we had children, we worked to make it the foundation of our choices as parents. For us, the bottom line on family was for us to cultivate and maintain:

- **Commitment to God:** Our faith came first in our lives. If we neglected or compromised that, nothing else would be of value.
- **Continual growth:** Reaching our personal potential and helping our children do the same is one of our highest values. When we come to the end of our lives, we want to look back knowing we lived life to the fullest.
- **Common experiences:** The greatest bonds between people come as the result of their experiences together, both good and bad. We create as many positive experiences as we can, and we weather the negative ones together.
- **Confidence—in God, ourselves, and others:** Your belief determines *how* you will live life, and it also affects the outcome of everything you do.
- **Contributions to life:** People should try to leave the world a better place than they found it. We want to add value not only to the people in our family, but also to every other life we touch.

As I said, this is our list. I'm not suggesting that you adopt our philosophy regarding family. I know you will want to create your own. Here's my suggestion: Keep it simple. If you come up with a list of seventeen things you want to live out, you won't be able to do it. You may not even be able to remember it! Whittle the list down to the nonnegotiables.

Develop Your Problem-Solving Strategy

I think a lot of people go into marriage expecting it to be easy. Maybe they've seen too many movies. Marriage isn't easy. Family isn't easy. Life isn't easy. Expect problems, stay committed, and develop a strategy for getting through the rough times. Some people call family meetings to discuss issues. Others create systems or rules.

My friends Kevin and Marcia Myers developed a system of fair fight rules after they had been married a few years. Kevin is very outgoing, energetic, and verbal, where Marcia is more quiet and reserved. Early in their marriage, he used to bulldoze right over her verbally. And they would get into marathon arguments.

So they decided on a set of rules to follow any time they got into a disagreement. One rule was that they would set an appointment to talk about an issue rather than picking at each other. Another was that Marcia *always* got to talk first. They've been married over twenty years, and their system has worked great for them.

Think about how you could improve your problem solving at home. Talk to your family members about it (during a calm time, not in the middle of a conflict). Use whatever kind of problem-solving strategy works for you. Just be sure that it fosters and promotes three things: (1) better understanding, (2) positive change, and (3) growing relationships.

MANAGING THE DISCIPLINE OF FAMILY

The desire to make your family a priority is one thing; actually living it out is something else. I found that it's often easier to get the approval of strangers and colleagues than it is to get respect from those who know you best. So I practice this discipline: ***Every day I work hard on gaining the love and respect of those closest to me.***

Years ago, when something exciting happened during the day or I heard a bit of interesting news, I'd share it with colleagues and friends. By the time I got home, I had little enthusiasm for sharing it with Margaret. So I purposely began keeping things to myself until I could share them with Margaret first. That way she never got the leftovers. I've found that the best way to place my family first is to give them some of my best energy and attention.

If you desire to strengthen your family life and make it a source of stability, then try practicing some of these disciplines:

Put Your Family on Your Calendar First

I have found that my work will gobble up every bit of my time if I let it. Before I made the decision to make my family a priority, I didn't give them the time I should have. I think that's true of most people who enjoy their careers. Other people have hobbies or interests that can be very time consuming. If you don't create boundaries for how you spend your time, your family will always get the leftovers. Even today, if I let my guard down, I'm liable to let work take over my schedule.

I battle that trend by putting my family on my calendar first. I block out weeks for family vacations. (That may sound too obvious to you, but I mention it because for the first several years I was married, we determined where we would vacation based on meeting people and going places that would benefit my work.) I schedule time with Margaret not only for us to go do things, like see a movie or a show, but also for us to simply be together. I devote time to our grandchildren. And when our children were young, I set aside time to attend ball games, recitals, and other activities.

Someone once said you should never let yourself feel that you ought to be at work when you're with your family, and you should never feel that you ought to be with your family when you're at work. That's a great perspective. If you and your family can figure out and agree on how much time you should spend together and you protect those times, you should be able to adopt that mind-set.

Create and Maintain Family Traditions

I want you to try an experiment. Get out a piece of paper and write down all the Christmas and birthday gifts you received when you were a kid up until you moved away from home. Take as much time as you need.

How many are you able to remember? There may be a handful that really stand out, but if you're like most people, you have a hard time recalling most of them. Now try this: List all the vacations you took with your family during those same years. Again, take as much time as you'd like.

I'd be willing to bet that if you took vacations every year, you were able to remember more of them than the presents you received. Why? Because what makes families happy isn't receiving things. It's doing things together. That's why I recommend establishing family traditions.

Traditions give your family a shared history and a strong sense of identity. Don't you remember how your family celebrated Thanksgiving as a child? How about Christmas? (And didn't you think yours was the *right* way when you got married and your spouse wanted to do something else?) The traditions your family kept helped you define who you were and who your family was.

Give thought to how you want to enjoy holidays, mark milestones, and celebrate rites of passage in your family. Start by basing traditions on your values. Add others you enjoyed from your childhood. If you're married, include those of your spouse as well. Mix in cultural elements if you want. Build some around your children's interests. Give traditions meaning and make them your own.

Find Ways to Spend Time Together

For a while, the family buzzwords were "quality time." But the truth is, no substitute exists for quantity of time. As psychiatrist Armand Nicholi says, "Time is like oxygen—there's a minimum amount that's necessary for survival. And it takes quantity as well as quality to develop warm and caring relationships."

Since busy, single-parent households are so common, and in the majority of two-parent families both parents work, you have to figure out ways to spend time together. For about six years when my children were teenagers, I gave up golf so that I would have more time available. And Margaret and I always worked especially hard to find time for certain things, such as

- **Significant events:** We made birthdays, ball games, recitals, and so forth important.
- **Significant needs:** You can't put a family member in crisis on hold.
- **Fun time:** We found that everybody relaxed and talked more when we were having fun.
- **One-on-one time:** Nothing lets another person know you care more than your undivided attention.

Come up with your own list of ways to spend time with your family.

Keep Your Marriage Healthy First

The relational foundation of any family is a couple's marriage. It sets the tone for the household, and it is the model relationship that children learn from more than any other. That's why former Notre Dame president Theodore Hesburgh asserted, "The most important thing a father can do for his children is love their mother."

No marriage is easy to keep going. It's been said that a successful marriage is one that can go from crisis to crisis with a growth in commitment. That's what it's really all about: commitment. Commitment is what carries you through. People who use their feelings as a barometer for the health of their marriage are destined for a breakup. If you intend to stay married only as long as you *feel* the love, you might as well give up. Just like anything else worth fighting for, marriage requires daily discipline and commitment.

Express Appreciation for Each Other

Psychologist William James said, "In every person from the cradle to the grave, there is a deep craving to be appreciated." If people don't receive affirmation and appreciation at home, there's a good chance they won't get it because, in general, the world does not fulfill that desire. One of the most positive things you can do for your spouse and children is really get to know them and love them simply because they are yours—not based on performance.

Resolve Conflict as Quickly as Possible

I've already mentioned how important it is to develop a strategy for resolving conflict, but it's such an important point that I want to remind you of it again. Every family has conflict, but not all families resolve it positively. A family's response to problems will either promote bonding or be destructive. Do it quickly and effectively, and you bring healing. Neglect conflict, and you may find yourself agreeing with novelist F. Scott Fitzgerald, who said, "Family quarrels are bitter things. They don't go according to any rules. They're not like aches or wounds, they're more like splits in the skin that won't heal because there's not enough material." It doesn't have to be that way.

Your Family Decision Today

Where do you stand when it comes to family today? Ask yourself these three questions:

1. Have I already made the decision to communicate with and care for my family?
2. If so, when did I make that decision?
3. What exactly did I decide?

Your Family Discipline Every Day

Based on the decision you made concerning family, what is the one discipline you must practice *today and every day* in order to be successful?

5

THINKING

I was very fortunate. I learned about the power of good thinking very early in life. My father required all three of his children to read for thirty minutes every day. Sometimes we chose what we read, but often he selected the reading material for us. Two of the books he asked me to read made a profound impression on me. The first was *The Power of Positive Thinking* by Norman Vincent Peale, which I read in the seventh grade.[10] That year, my father also took me to Veterans Memorial Auditorium in Columbus, Ohio, to hear and meet Dr. Peale. It shaped my life.

Even more important than meeting Dr. Peale was reading *As a Man Thinketh* by James Allen.[11] I read the book in 1961 when I was fourteen years old, and it made such an impression on me that I was prompted to make one of my Daily Dozen decisions. I still have the book. On page 49, Allen wrote, "All that a man achieves or fails to achieve is the direct result of his thoughts." The entire book made an impression on me, but that statement made me realize that my thinking would make or break me. So I decided, *I will think on things that will add value to myself and others.*

MAKING THE DECISION TO PRACTICE AND DEVELOP GOOD THINKING DAILY

If you desire to make good thinking a daily part of your life, consider this:

Understand That Great Thinking Comes from Good Thinking

One night at dinner, a friend of John Kilcullen's described something he overheard in a bookstore. A customer asked the clerk, "Do you have any simple books on Microsoft DOS—something like DOS for dummies?" It was only a passing comment, meant as a joke. But it stuck with Kilcullen. And he did something with it. He launched the "Dummies" books.

Some unknown consumer had a good idea, and it went nowhere. In fact, he probably didn't even know his idea was a good one. But in the hands of a thinker, that good idea became a great idea. Then it became a bunch of great ideas. The "Dummies" books now encompass a product line of 370 titles in thirty-one languages with sales of more than 60 million copies.[12]

If you want to become a great thinker, you first need to become a good thinker. Before becoming a good thinker, you need to become a thinker. In order to become a thinker, you need to be willing to first produce a bunch of mediocre and downright bad ideas. Only by practicing and developing your thinking daily will your ideas get better. Your thinking ability is determined not by your desire to think, but by your past thinking. To become a good thinker, do more thinking. Once the ideas start flowing, they get better. Once they get better, they keep improving.

Recognize There Are Many Kinds of Thinking

Up to now I've referred to thinking as if it were a single skill. But the truth is that it's really a collection of skills. It's like a mental decathlon, the track-and-field contest where athletes compete in ten events: 100-meter dash, 400-meter dash, long jump, shot put, high jump, 110-meter hurdles, discus throw, pole vault, javelin throw, and 1,500-meter run. Thinking is multifaceted.

I believe eleven different thinking skills come into play when it comes to good thinking. I wrote about them in detail in *Thinking for a Change*. Here is an overview of the skills:

1. **Big picture thinking:** the ability to think beyond yourself and your world in order to process ideas with a holistic perspective
2. **Focused thinking:** the ability to think with clarity on issues by removing distractions and mental clutter from your mind
3. **Creative thinking:** the ability to break out of your

"box" of limitations and explore ideas and options to experience a breakthrough

4. **Realistic thinking:** the ability to build a solid foundation on facts to think with certainty

5. **Strategic thinking:** the ability to implement plans that give direction for today and increase your potential for tomorrow

6. **Possibility thinking:** the ability to unleash your enthusiasm and hope to find solutions for even seemingly impossible situations

7. **Reflective thinking:** the ability to revisit the past in order to gain a true perspective and think with understanding

8. **Questioning popular thinking:** the ability to reject the limitations of common thinking and accomplish uncommon results

9. **Shared thinking:** the ability to include the heads of others to help you think "over your head" and achieve compounding results

10. **Unselfish thinking:** the ability to consider others and their journey to think with collaboration

11. **Bottom-line thinking:** the ability to focus on results and maximum return to reap the full potential of your thinking[13]

It's a real mistake to believe there is only one kind of thinking. That's a very narrow view. It can cause a person to value only the kind of thinking in which he excels and to dismiss all other types of thinking. I'm sorry to say that some academicians fall into this trap.

Maximize Your Strengths and Staff Your Weaknesses

Most people are naturally good at a few thinking skills and weak at others. Just as it's rare to find an athlete who is good enough in all ten events to compete in the decathlon, it's a rare thinker who has skill in all eleven thinking areas. So if you recognize that there are many different kinds of thinking, what should you do? Should you try to master all of them? No, I believe that's a mistake.

Let's say, for example, that you are a very good creative thinker, but you're weak in bottom-line thinking, yet you want to master both kinds of thinking. How would you get started? Where would you focus your attention? You could probably work on bottom-line thinking to get it up to average, but that would require a tremendous amount of time, energy, and resources. And what would it take to advance to merely good? It would take even more effort. The higher you try to climb, the more energy it takes to make less progress. No matter how hard you try, you might not ever make bottom-line thinking a strength.

What if you gave that time to improving your creative thinking instead? Since you are already good, a moderate amount of time and energy could make you excellent. If you really gave it your all, perhaps you could become a world-class creative thinker. That would enable you to generate ideas and make contributions few others could. That would make you much more valuable and give you a real advantage in your life and career.

So what do you do about your weaknesses? Gather people around you who are strong in those areas. That's what I've done for years. In my current season of life, I can hire staff who possess strengths in my areas of weakness. But even before I was "the boss," I practiced this principle. For thirty-five years my wife, Margaret, and I have worked as a team to compensate for each other's weaknesses. I've often relied on my brother, Larry, to help me in the area of realistic thinking. And I've made it a practice to partner with friends who think better than I do in a particular area while I do the same for them. Not having to rely entirely on myself when it comes to thinking has been a real advantage for me.

MANAGING THE DISCIPLINE OF THINKING

It's easy to allow situations and other people to influence your thinking negatively as well as positively. One of the tricky things about seeking ideas and perspective from others is that some people have an agenda other than helping you. That's why it's important to take responsibility for your own thinking. When I was in my twenties, I began to practice this discipline: *Every day I will set aside a time to think, and I will determine to think on the right things.* If you desire to do the same thing, then do the following:

Find a Place to Think

Beginning with my first job in 1969, I've always found a place to be my daily thinking spot. During those early years in Hillham, Indiana, it was beside a spring outside our home. In Lancaster, Ohio, I used to sit on a big rock. In San Diego, it was an isolated room upstairs at the church. In Atlanta, it's a particular chair in my office. The only time I sit in it is when I need thinking time.

Those certainly haven't been the only places I've done my thinking, but they are the ones I've designated for the task. But I can make almost any place a good thinking place as long as I don't have to deal with interruptions. Right now as I write this, I'm sitting in a chair on the balcony of a cruise ship. My family is scattered all over the ship doing different things, and I sneaked away for a few minutes by myself to think about this book and write down some ideas.

I want to encourage you to find a thinking place. When it comes to what works, everybody's different. Some people like to be connected to nature. Others want to be in the midst of—but removed from—activity. My friend Andy Stanley likes to sit alone in a restaurant to think—he says he needs a little distraction. J. K. Rowling, author of the "Harry Potter" books, wrote her early books while sitting in a café. Where you go doesn't matter as long as it stimulates your thinking.

Set Aside Think Time Every Day

As important as finding the right place to think is carving out the time. I do nearly all my best thinking early in the morning—except for reflective thinking. I usually do that in the evenings before I go to bed. That's when I review my day and try to measure how I did with my Daily Dozen. But all the other kinds of thinking come best to me in the morning. I often wake up in the wee hours and spend time just jotting ideas on a legal pad while sitting in my thinking chair. I recommend that you try to discover the time of day when your thinking is the sharpest. Then set aside a block of time every day just to think. I believe you'll find that you're much more productive and focused as a result.

Find a Process That Works for You

Everybody has a different way of approaching the process of thinking. Poet Rudyard Kipling had to have pure black ink for his pen before he could write. Philosopher Immanuel Kant used to stare out his window at a stone tower to think; when trees grew up threatening to block his view, he chopped them down. Composer Ludwig van Beethoven poured cold water over his head to refresh himself and stimulate his thinking. Poet Friedrich von Schiller's thinking was stimulated by the smell of rotting apples, which he kept on his desk. Critic and lexicographer Samuel Johnson said that he needed a purring cat, an orange peel, and a cup of tea in order to write. Composer Gioacchino Rossini felt that he worked best in bed under the covers.

I don't need anything specific to trigger my thinking. Some people need music. Some think best while at a computer. Some must write in longhand. Do whatever works for you.

Capture Your Thoughts

If you don't write down your ideas, there is a great danger you will lose them. In *Bird by Bird,* Anne Lamott explains how she keeps from losing her best ideas:

> I have index cards and pens all over the house—by the bed, in the bathroom, in the kitchen, by the phones, and I have them in the glove compartment of my car. I carry one with me in my back pocket when I take my dog for a walk. . . . I used to think that if something was important enough, I'd remember it until I got home, where I could simply write it down in my notebook. . . . But then I wouldn't. . . . [Writing down your ideas right away is] not cheating. It doesn't say anything about your character.[14]

I always write down my ideas. When I'm in my thinking spot, I use a legal pad. The rest of the day, I keep a small leather-bound notebook with me. I even have something to write with next to my bed at night: a small pad with a light attached that illuminates when you remove the pen. That way, I can write a note while still in bed without disturbing Margaret by turning on a light. Have a system and use it.

Put Your Thoughts into Action Quickly

When you have a great idea but don't do anything with it, then you don't reap the advantage it brings. Dave Goetz, founder of CustomZines.com, says, "For me, when an idea hits me, it strikes fire, almost like God speaking. I know that sounds heretical, but there it is. The more time that passes after the idea strikes, the less heat it gives off. I forget parts of it, it doesn't seem as great. Ideas have a short half-life."[15]

Have you ever had an idea for a product or service and a few months or years later seen someone else with the same idea take it to market? Author Alfred Montapert said, "Every time a person puts an idea across, he finds ten people who thought about it *before* he did—but they only *thought* about it." Ideas, put into action, give an advantage.

Try to Improve Your Thinking Every Day

It's true that the more thinking you do, the better you become at it. But you can quickly improve your thinking if you do the following on a daily basis:

- **Focus on the positive:** Thinking alone won't guarantee success. You need to think about the right things. Negative thinking and worry actually hinder the thinking process rather than improve it. I believe in this so wholeheartedly that the first book I wrote was a collection of short, uplifting, and instructive chapters. I called it *Think on These Things*, based on a Bible passage that always inspired me: "Whatever is true, whatever is honorable, whatever is just, whatever is pure, whatever is pleasing, whatever is commendable, if there is any excellence and if there is anything worthy of praise, think about these things."[16] Focus on the positive, and your thinking will move in a positive direction.

- **Gather good input:** I've always been a collector of ideas. I do a lot of reading, and I continually file the ideas and quotations I find. I've found that the more good ideas I'm exposed to, the more my thinking improves.

- **Spend time with good thinkers:** If you were to interview a group of top executives in any profession, you would find that well over half had the benefit of being mentored at some time in their careers. And I believe that the greatest benefit anyone receives in that kind of relationship is learning how the mentor thinks. If you spend time with good thinkers, you will find that the exposure sharpens your thinking.

I believe that many people take thinking for granted. They see it as a natural function of life. But the truth is that *intentional* thinking isn't commonplace. What you do every day in the area of thinking really matters because it sets the stage for all your actions, and it will bring you either adversity or advantage.

Your Thinking Decision Today

Where do you stand when it comes to thinking today? Ask yourself these three questions:

1. Have I already made the decision to practice and develop good thinking daily?
2. If so, when did I make that decision?
3. What exactly did I decide?

Your Thinking Discipline Every Day

Based on the decision you made concerning thinking, what is the one discipline you must practice *today and every day* in order to be successful?

6

COMMITMENT

I don't think I really understood the true value of commitment until 1976. I was the senior pastor of one of the fastest-growing churches in Ohio. And the success we were seeing necessitated a $1 million expansion of our facilities. But there was a problem: I was only twenty-nine years old, and I had never led a major building program. Frankly, the task seemed impossible. But at the same time, the future of the church absolutely depended on its success. That's when I made a life decision concerning commitment: *If something is worth doing, I will commit myself to carrying it through.* I decided that come what might, I would lead my congregation through the building program.

Little did I realize how much that commitment would be tested. Each time we made a decision, more problems arose. Here are just a few:

1. To accommodate the growth, I needed to improve my

staff. That meant terminating some people who were very popular.

2. More than two hundred people in the church (nearly 15 percent) left the church because they did not agree with the vision.

3. Our bank agreed to lend us the money only if we first raised $300,000 from among the congregation, but I had never led a large financial campaign, and the most I had ever raised for a project was $25,000.

4. The church board's decision not to give the bid for the building contract to a member of our congregation who owned a construction company caused him to leave the church, and he had been the church's most generous giver.

5. Our architect was careless with disbursements to contractors, which made the project cost over $125,000 more than it should have.

You've heard the old saying that motion causes friction? During the entire process, there was enough friction to cause a five-alarm fire. I felt like I was in the hot seat every day. If I hadn't made the commitment early in the process, I never would have made it through.

MAKING THE DECISION TO MAKE AND KEEP PROPER COMMITMENTS DAILY

If you desire to have greater tenacity to accomplish the things you desire, then make the decision to embrace commitment wholeheartedly in your life. Begin by doing the following:

Count the Cost

After the Nazis drove the British army from the European continent at Dunkirk and obtained France's surrender in June 1940, the Germans were certain that victory in Europe was at hand and that Great Britain would seek a peace agreement. France also believed that was true. French General Maxime Weygand told Charles de Gaulle, who was a colonel at the time, "When I've been beaten here, England won't wait a week before negotiating with the Reich."[17]

But the Germans and the French underestimated the commitment of Winston Churchill, who had become England's prime minister in May, and of the British people. Churchill knew what was at stake in the conflict, as evidenced by his remarks at the time:

What General Weygand called the Battle of France is over. I expect that the battle of Britain is about to begin. Upon this battle depends the survival of Christian civilisation. Upon it depends our own British life. . . . Hitler knows that he will have to break us in this island or lose the war. If we can stand up to him, all Europe may be free. . . . But if we fail, then the whole world, including the United States, including all that we have known and cared for, will sink into the abyss of a new dark age. . . . Let us therefore brace ourselves to our duties, and so bear ourselves that, if the British Empire and its Commonwealth last for a thousand years, men will still say, "This was their finest hour."[18]

The war that England fought was long and bloody. They suffered terrible bombing from the Nazis, and for a long time they stood alone. But they stood. Their commitment was unwavering. And because they stood, the Allies won the war. I believe their resolve was strong not only because they knew what was at stake, but also because they had a sense of what price they were being asked to pay. It can be very difficult to stand by a commitment naively made. The commitment becomes much stronger when you have already counted the cost.

Determine to Pay the Price

Once you count the cost, then you have to decide whether you are really willing to do what it takes to follow through. U.S. senator Sam Nunn said, "You have to pay the price. You will find that everything in life exacts a price, and you will have to decide whether the price is worth the prize."

When I went off to college, I was determined to stay committed and focused on preparing for the ministry. But I knew there would be a price. Many of my college friends got married while still in school, and some even had children; Margaret and I waited, despite our shared desire to begin our married life. It was a difficult journey. And to this day, I don't recommend engagements as long as ours. But our commitment paid off. A few weeks after we graduated, we got married. And we waited several years before having children. As a result, I was prepared when I entered the ministry, and I could focus on establishing my career during those important early years.

Always Strive for Excellence

Howard W. Newton said, "People forget how fast you did a job—but they remember how well you did it." Few things fire up a person's commitment like dedication to excellence. The desire for excellence carried Michelangelo through to the completion of his work on the Sistine Chapel. Excellence drove Edison to keep trying until he figured out how to make a lightbulb that worked. Excellence drives the companies Jim Collins wrote about in *Built to Last* and *Good to Great.*

Anyone who desires to achieve and become successful must be like a fine craftsman: committed to excellence. A great craftsman wants you to inspect his work, to look closely at its finest details. In contrast, sloppy people hide their work. And if anyone finds fault with it, shoddy workers find fault with their tools. Which are you most like? Excellence means doing your very best in everything, in every way. That kind of commitment will take you where halfhearted people will never go.

MANAGING THE DISCIPLINE OF COMMITMENT

After I made the decision to commit myself to the building program at my church, I knew that I would need to find a way to keep myself on track. So I determined to live

out this discipline: ***Every day I will renew my commitment
and think about the benefits that come from it.*** To do that,
I carried a laminated card with me every day for eighteen
months. Here's what was written on it:

> The moment one definitely commits oneself, then
> Providence moves too. All sorts of things occur to help
> one that would never otherwise have occurred. A whole
> stream of events issue from the decision, raising in one's
> favor all manner of unforeseen incidents and meet-
> ings and material assistance which no man could have
> dreamed would come his way.—William H. Murray

I read that card every day as we were going through the
project. On especially difficult days when I felt like throw-
ing in the towel, I read it two or three times. It helped me to
stay focused and feel encouraged. I thought, If I stay committed and do all I can, and then I ask God to make up the
difference, we can achieve this. And we did!

When you accomplish something that you once believed
was impossible, it makes you a new person. It changes the
way you see yourself and the world. My thinking went to
a new level, and the vision for my leadership expanded. I
never would have gotten there without commitment. My
personal commitment—and that of many others—was the
key to our success.

As you strive to keep your commitments daily, keep the
following in mind:

Expect Commitment to Be a Struggle

When our children were young and living at home, Margaret and I decided one summer we wanted to take them on a vacation that focused on how the United States was built as a nation. We started out in New York City. We went to Ellis Island, the longtime gateway into the country, and got a feel for the millions of immigrants who came to America with the dream of building a better life. We visited Philadelphia. We saw the room where our country became a nation with the signing of the Declaration of Independence. We viewed the Liberty Bell. And we visited the graves of the brave men who signed the Declaration of Independence.

After that, we traveled south to Williamsburg, Virginia, the home of Patrick Henry, who declared, "Give me liberty or give me death!" And we ended the trip in Washington, D.C. As we looked up at the towering Washington Monument, we were reminded of the United States' struggle to become a nation. As we gazed at the huge statue of Lincoln at his memorial, we recalled the struggle we have endured to *remain* a nation.

Everywhere we went, we were confronted with the commitment of the men and women who founded and preserved our country. We learned about the risks they took, the battles they fought, the sacrifices they made. The greatest honors were reserved for those who endured the greatest struggles. The stakes were high, but so were the rewards. We still enjoy the freedom they won for us.

That trip taught a great lesson to our family. Anything worth having is going to be a struggle. Commitment doesn't come easy, but when you're fighting for something you believe in, the struggle is worth it.

Don't Rely on Talent Alone

If you want to reach your potential, you need to add a strong work ethic to your talent. Poet Henry Wadsworth Longfellow shared much insight when he wrote:

> The heights by great men reached and kept
> Were not attained by sudden flight,
> But they, while their companions slept,
> Were toiling upward in the night.[19]

If you want something out of your day, you must put something in it. Your talent is what God put in before you were born. Your skills are what you put in yesterday. Commitment is what you must put in today in order to make today your masterpiece and make tomorrow a success.

Focus on Choices, Not Conditions

In general, people approach daily commitment in one of two ways. They focus on the external or the internal. Those who focus on the external expect conditions to determine whether they keep their commitments. Because conditions are so transitory, their commitment level changes like the wind.

In contrast, people who base their actions on the internal usually focus on their choices. Each choice is a crossroad, one that will either confirm or compromise their commitments.

When you come to a crossroad, you can recognize it because:

- A personal decision is required.
- The decision will cost you something.
- Others will likely be influenced by it.

Your choices are the only thing you truly control. You cannot control your circumstances, nor can you control others'. By focusing on your choices, and then making them with integrity, you control your commitment. And that is what often separates success from failure.

Be Single-minded

Nothing stokes commitment like single-minded effort that results in achievement. A great example of that truth can be found in the story of English minister William Carey. Although he had only an elementary education, by the time Carey was in his teens, he could read the Bible in six languages. Because of his talent for languages, when he was in his early thirties he was chosen to be a missionary to India. Six years later, in 1799, he founded the Serampore mission. A few years after that, he became professor of Oriental languages at Fort William College in Calcutta. He also used his talent with languages in becoming a publisher. His press at Serampore printed Bibles in forty languages and dialects for more than three hundred million people.

To what did Carey attribute his success? How was he able to accomplish what he did? He said it was because he was a "plodder." Describing himself, Carey said, "Anything beyond this will be too much. I can plod. That is my only genius. I can persevere in any definite pursuit. To this I owe everything."[20]

Do What's Right Even When You Don't Feel Like It

Thomas A. Buckner said, "To bring one's self to a frame of mind and to the proper energy to accomplish things that require plain hard work continuously is the one big battle that everyone has. When this battle is won for all time, then everything is easy." One of the things I admire about great athletes is their understanding of this truth. That's one of the reasons I enjoy watching the Olympics. When the Olympic athletes come into the stadium during the opening ceremonies and prepare to participate in the games, one of the things they do is recite the following:

> I have prepared.
> I have followed the rules.
> I will not quit.

Anyone who can say that with integrity can be proud of him- or herself, no matter what happens afterward. As Arthur Gordon, author of *A Touch of Wonder*, said, "Nothing is easier than saying words. Nothing is harder than living them, day after day. What you promise today must be renewed and redecided tomorrow and each day that stretches out before you."[21]

If you do what you should only when you *really* feel

like it, you won't keep your commitments consistently. My friend Ken Blanchard says, "When you're interested in something, you do it only when it's convenient. When you're committed to something, you accept no excuses, only results." If you refuse to give in to excuses, no matter how good they may sound or how good they will make you feel in the moment, you have the potential to go far.

Your Commitment Decision Today

Where do you stand when it comes to commitment today? Ask yourself these three questions:

1. Have I already made the decision to make and keep proper commitments daily?
2. If so, when did I make that decision?
3. What exactly did I decide?

Your Commitment Discipline Every Day

Based on the decision you made concerning commitment, what is the one discipline you must practice *today and every day* in order to be successful?

7

FINANCES

When I was growing up, it was obvious very early that my brother, Larry, and I had very different attitudes toward money. We were complete opposites. As a kid, all Larry wanted to do was work and make money. All I wanted to do was play with my friends. He spent his summers working. I spent my summers shooting hoops. He saved his money. I had nothing to save. When Larry was sixteen years old, he bought himself a nice car with his own money: a four-year-old Ford. I didn't have a car until I graduated from college. It was an old beat-up Ford Falcon—and guess from whom I borrowed the money to buy it. From Larry—and from my younger sister, Trish.

When I was studying for the ministry, I realized I was choosing a profession in which I would not make a lot of money. I didn't mind that because I was doing what I believed I was called to do and what would be personally fulfilling. But I also recognized that when a person has no money, he has few options. In 1985, Margaret and I made a decision: *We will sacrifice today so that we can have options tomorrow.* From then on, we've determined to live by this financial formula:

- 10 percent to church/charity
- 10 percent to investments
- 80 percent to living expenses

Around that same time, our friend Tom Phillippe offered us a wonderful opportunity to invest in one of his retirement centers. We gladly accepted. For several years, we've not only continued to put 10 percent of our income into investments, but when those investments have made money, instead of spending it, we have rolled it over into other investments. Over time our money has been building. And the older Margaret and I get, the more options we have as a result.

MAKING THE DECISION TO EARN AND PROPERLY MANAGE FINANCES DAILY

If you desire to have options, yet you have not done a good job of earning and properly managing your finances daily, then put yourself in position to make a good decision concerning finances by doing the following:

Put the Value of Things into Perspective

A husband and wife attended a county fair where a man in an old biplane was giving rides for $50. The couple wanted to ride, but they thought the pilot's price was too high. They tried negotiating to get him to lower the price, offering $50 for them both, but he wouldn't budge. Finally, the pilot made them an offer.

"You pay me the whole $100, and I'll take you up," he said. "And if you don't say a single word during the flight, I'll give you back all your money."

They agreed, and the couple got into the plane. Up they went, and the pilot proceeded to do every aerial maneuver he knew: diving, looping, rolling, and flying upside down. When the plane landed, the pilot said to the husband, "Congratulations! Here's your $100. You didn't say a word."

"Nope," answered the husband, "but I almost did when my wife fell out."

It's a hokey story, but it directs us to a truth about our culture. People tend to value money and things over what's really important in life: other people. French historian and political scientist Alexis de Tocqueville remarked about the United States that he knew of "no other country where love of money has such a grip on men's hearts." Remarkably, he wrote that more than one hundred years ago! I wonder what he would say if he were alive today.

To know whether your attitude about money and possessions is what it should be, ask yourself the following five questions:

1. Am I preoccupied with things?
2. Am I envious of others?
3. Do I find my personal value in possessions?

4. Do I believe that money will make me happy?
5. Do I continually want more?

If you answered yes to one or more of these questions, you need to do some soul-searching. Billy Graham rightly points out, "If a person gets his attitude toward money straight, it will help straighten out almost every other area of his life." Materialism is a mind-set. There's nothing wrong with possessing money or nice things. Likewise, there's nothing wrong with living modestly. Materialism is not about possession—it's an obsession. I've known materialistic people with no money and nonmaterialistic people who possess lots of money. Haven't you?

Recognize Your Season of Life

Not every phase of life is the same, nor should we try to make it that way. Ideally, a person's life should follow a pattern where the main focus goes from learning to earning to returning. Here's what I mean about each phase:

- **Learn:** When you're young, your focus should be on exploring your talents, discovering your purpose, and learning your trade. For many people, this phase occurs during their teens and twenties—although a few trailblazers do it earlier and some late bloomers don't have things worked out until well into their thirties (or later). The exact timing isn't important. What matters is that you accept that there is a phase of life where learning is your primary objective and that you shouldn't take shortcuts to financial gain and miss the big picture of your life.

- **Earn:** If you're on track with your purpose, you've learned your trade well, and you practice it with excellence, the hope is that you will be able to earn a good living. Obviously, your choice of profession affects your earning power greatly. For many people, the season when their earning is most effective occurs during their thirties, forties, and fifties. During this phase of life, you should strive to take care of your family and prepare for your future.

- **Return:** We should always try to be generous, no matter our age. But if you've worked hard and planned well, you may enter a phase of life that is most rewarding, where you can focus on giving back to others. Most often, that occurs when people are in their fifties, sixties, seventies, and beyond. Margaret and I are planning how we hope to do that in the coming years.

Obviously these phases are generalizations, but they present a pattern for which to strive. If you are young, then you may be eager to leave the learning phase. Be patient, because the more diligently you go after phase one, the greater your potential to maximize the other phases. If you're older and you didn't lay a good foundation for yourself, don't despair. Keep learning and growing. You still have a chance to finish well. But if you give up, you'll never go up.

Reduce Your Debt

Michael Kidwell and Steve Rhode, authors of *Get Out of Debt: Smart Solutions to Your Money Problems,* believe, "Every person in debt is suffering from some type of depression. Debt is one of the leading causes of divorce, lack of sleep, and poor work performance. It is truly one of the deep dark secrets that people have. It robs them of their self-worth and keeps them from achieving dreams."[22]

Going into debt for things that appreciate in value can be a good idea. Purchasing a house, securing transportation so you can work, improving your education, and investing in a business are good things—as long as you can manage them well. But many people incur debt for frivolous things. When you're still paying for something you no longer use or even have, it means trouble.

Kidwell and Rhode suggest five steps to reduce debt:

1. Stop incurring debt.
2. Track your cash.
3. Plan for the future.
4. Don't expect instant miracles.
5. Seek professional help.[23]

Don't let your possessions or your lifestyle possess you. If you're a slave to debt, find a way to free yourself.

Put Your Financial Formula into Place

Someone once observed that the difference between the rich and the poor is that the rich invest their money and spend what's left, while the poor spend their money and invest what's left. If you haven't decided to plan your finances, you're headed for trouble. Put yourself on a budget. Create a financial formula that works for you. You may want to try the 10-10-80 approach that we use. But do something! The old saying is corny but true: Failing to plan is like planning to fail.

MANAGING THE DISCIPLINE OF FINANCES

I have to admit that money has never been my number-one motivation in life. Truthfully, finances were so low on my list of priorities that for a time I neglected them, which is probably why I didn't make my good life decision concerning finances until I was in my late thirties. But we've all seen what lack of good financial management can do to people in their twilight years. Recently my son-in-law, Steve, and I went to eat at a restaurant when we were down in Florida, and a lovely lady in her midseventies waited on us. Now, you never know another person's situation; some people work into their eighties simply for the joy of work or to be with people. But I know that the majority of people who keep working in physically demanding jobs during that season of life do it because they have no other choice. My friend financial expert Ron Blue says that the average annual income for people over age sixty-five is $6,300.[24] In the case of our waitress, I sensed that she worked because she had no other options. So Steve and I left her a great tip. The next time you find yourself being waited on by senior citizens, you might want to do something for them.

I'm still growing in the discipline of finances. I settled my personal financial issue years ago with 10-10-80, but it's been only in the last decade that I've learned to be better at finances in business. I used to focus on the vision for the organization, hire the best leaders I could find to join me in achieving it, and then lead to the best of my ability. I pretty much left the financial aspects of the business to others. But my brother, Larry, took me to task for that attitude. He told me that I had no right to neglect business finances just because it wasn't an area of strength or passion for me. So now, at home and in business, I maintain this discipline: ***Every day I will focus on my financial game plan so that each day I will have more, not fewer, options.*** The earlier you make the decision and practice the discipline of sound financial management, the more options you will have.

To help you approach your finances every day with the right attitude, do the following:

Become a Good Earner

To become a good financial manager, you must first have something to manage. That's why I believe the first discipline of finances is to maximize your earning potential. By that I don't mean to neglect the other important areas of life in order to make a buck. Nor am I suggesting that your focus should always be on money. Just maintain a strong work ethic and learn how to make and manage money. Develop relationships with people who are successful in this area and learn from them. There are also plenty of good books about personal and business finances.

Work ethic, on the other hand, is more about desire than knowledge. It comes from within. Anything can fuel that desire: the passion to serve others, the promise of escaping the circumstances of our birth, a vision for progress, or a personal passion. What often puts out the fire of desire is the belief that the work is too great for the return.

If you find yourself thinking that you have it especially hard in your job or career, you might need to put things into perspective. Take a look at the rules that employees at Mt. Corry Carriage and Iron Works were asked to follow in 1872:

1. Employees will daily sweep the floors, dust the furniture, shelves, and showcases.
2. Each day fill lamps, clean chimneys and trim wicks, wash windows once a week.
3. Each clerk will bring a bucket of water and a scuttle of coal for the day's business.
4. Make your pens carefully. You may whittle nibs to individual taste.
5. This office will open at 7 a.m. and close at 8 p.m. daily except on the Sabbath.
6. Men employees will be given an evening off each week for courting purposes, or two evenings if they go regularly to church.
7. Every employee should lay aside from each pay a goodly sum of his earnings for his benefit during his

declining years so that he will not become a burden upon the charity of his betters.

8. Any employee who smokes Spanish cigars, uses liquor in any form, gets shaved at a barber shop, or frequents public halls will give good reason to suspect his worth, intentions, integrity, and honesty.

9. The employee who has performed his labors faithfully and without fault for a period of five years in my service and who has been thrifty and attentive to his religious duties and is looked upon by his fellow-man as a substantial and law-abiding citizen will be given an increase of 5 cents per day in his pay, providing that just returns in profits from the business permit.

We enjoy a lot of advantages today that people didn't have in previous generations. One of them is that we don't have to fulfill the same expectations of those in previous centuries. With the right attitude and a willingness to pay the price, almost anyone can pursue nearly any opportunity and achieve it.

Be Grateful Every Day

One of the most important things you can do for yourself is keep your perspective and be thankful for whatever you have. Poet Rudyard Kipling once told his audience while speaking at a graduation ceremony, "Do not pay too much attention to fame, power, or money. Some day you will meet a person who cares for none of these, and then you will know how poor you are." If you work hard and maintain an attitude of gratitude, you'll find it easier to manage your finances every day.

Don't Compare Yourself to Others

Whenever people start comparing themselves to others, they get into trouble. Comparisons of money and possessions can be especially detrimental. Wanting to keep up with neighbors or appear well-off gets many people into horrible debt. *New Yorker* financial writer James Surowiecki says, "Americans have always been stricken by the disease that some have called 'luxury fever' or 'affluenza.' Even if we aren't rich yet, we'd like to look as if we were."[25]

If you see your neighbors buying new furnishings for their home, taking elaborate vacations, and driving a new vehicle every year, does something stir inside you to do the same? That someone *appears* to be in circumstances similar to yours doesn't mean anything. Your neighbors might earn twice as much as you do. Or they may be in debt up to their eyeballs and three-fourths of the way to bankruptcy court. Don't make assumptions, and don't try to be like someone else.

Give as Much as You Can

Author Bruce Larson says, "Money is another pair of hands to heal and feed and bless the desperate families of the earth. . . . In other words, money is my other self. Money can go where I do not have time to go, where I do not have a passport to go. My money can go in my place and heal and bless and feed and help. A man's money is an extension of himself." That's true of your money only if you're willing to part with it. Or to put it a more colorful way, as Hanna Andersson Clothing company founder Gun Denhart did: "Money is like manure. If you let it pile up, it just smells. But if you spread it around, you can encourage things to grow."

My brother, Larry, recently gave me this quotation from Blaise Pascal: "I love poverty because Jesus loved it. I love wealth because it affords me the means of helping the needy. I keep faith with everyone." I've mentioned "options" a lot in this chapter. That may seem like a selfish word to you. But I have to tell you, for me having options is about service. Philanthropist Andrew Carnegie said his goal was to spend the first half of his life accumulating wealth and the second half giving it away. What a great idea! My desire is to spend my future years giving to others. I won't be able to give on the scale that Carnegie did, but that's not important. What matters is that I do what I can by practicing financial discipline.

Your Financial Decision Today

Where do you stand when it comes to finances today? Ask yourself these three questions:

1. Have I already made the decision to earn and properly manage my finances daily?
2. If so, when did I make that decision?
3. What exactly did I decide?

Your Financial Discipline Every Day

Based on the decision you made concerning finances, what is the one discipline you must practice *today and every day* in order to be successful?

8

FAITH

I grew up in a household filled with faith. My father, Melvin, became a pastor as a young man and remains in ministry to this day at age eighty-three. I heard words of faith from him and my mother, Laura, every day growing up. But you can't live on someone else's faith. There are no spiritual grandchildren. Each person must make his own decision and act on it with integrity. At age seventeen, I made my faith decision: *I will accept God's gift of his Son, Jesus Christ, as my Savior.*

That decision, more than any other, has shaped my life. It has forged my worldview. Recognition of God's love for everyone has influenced how I view others. The Golden Rule has taught me how to treat people. God's love for me has given me great self-worth. And the Bible has taught me how to lead people. Whenever I am asked to sign a copy of the *Maxwell Leadership Bible*, the edition that contains leadership notes from my thirty years of studying leadership in Scripture, I write, "Everything I know about leadership I learned from this Book."

It is my privilege to be a national board member of the Center for Faith Walk Leadership. The organization, founded by my friend Ken Blanchard, encourages leading in the workplace according to the highest standard. Here's what Ken says that means:

> It doesn't mean the bottom line, or looking good to Wall Street, or being praised by your peers. It's not about getting the credit, or the promotions, or the raises. It's about working with those you lead to get results in a way that honors God. It's about people, service, and results. It's a new way of leading based on the teachings of Jesus, the greatest leader of all time. He gave his followers a vision of something greater than themselves. He consistently reminded them of the long-term effects of their work. He allowed those around him to fail, but held them accountable. He redirected them. He forgave them, and he inspired the best in others. And the result? He started a movement that continues to thrive more than 2,000 years later.

True leadership starts with the heart—with character. The underlying message from God is not to act differently, but to become different. Not to act honestly, but to become an honest person. Then honesty will be at the core of your leadership style. It will be at the core of your life. My faith has not only given me peace; it has given me a wonderful model for leadership and life.

MAKING THE DECISION TO DEEPEN AND LIVE OUT FAITH DAILY

If you desire to make an honest exploration of faith, then know this:

We Already Have Faith . . . The Important Choice Is Where We Place It

Author John Bisagno observed, "Faith is at the heart of life. You go to a doctor whose name you cannot pronounce. He gives you a prescription you cannot read. You take it to a pharmacist you have never seen. He gives you a medicine you do not understand and yet you take it."

We all have faith. Every day we act on beliefs that have little or no evidence to back them up. That is also true in a spiritual sense. Just as one person has faith that God is real, an atheist has faith that there is no God. Both people hold strong beliefs, and neither person can produce evidence to absolutely prove his point of view. Right now, you already have faith in something. Your goal should be to align your beliefs with the truth. Seek the truth, and I believe you will find it.

Understand That Faith Is Often Birthed Out of Difficulties

I've already shared that some skeptical people see faith as a negative thing, almost as a sign of weakness. If faith is new to you and you are uncertain how to approach it, then I would advise you to view it as an opportunity for a course correction in the journey of life. In a play by T. S. Eliot, one of the most influential poets of the twentieth century, one character expresses it in those terms. He describes a faith that comes after extreme disappointment. He calls it the "kind of faith that arises after despair. The destination cannot be described; you will know very little until you get there; you will journey blind. But the way leads toward possession of what you have sought for in the wrong place."

If you are experiencing difficulties, allow yourself to explore faith in response to it. Henri Nouwen said this "is the great conversation in our life: to recognize and believe that the many unexpected events are not just disturbing interruptions of our projects, but the way in which God molds our hearts and prepares us." Faith not only can help you through a crisis, it can help you to approach life after the hard times with a whole new perspective. It can help you adopt an outlook of hope and courage through faith to face reality.

A Faith That Hasn't Been Tested Can't Be Trusted

It's not enough to simply make a faith decision. If you want to live it out, then you have to work at deepening it. Faith gives you peace and strength only if it's not superficial. The deeper the faith, the greater its potential to carry you through the rough times. As Rabbi Abraham Heschel said, "Faith like Job's cannot be shaken because it is the result of having been shaken."

Perhaps nothing in recent history tested the faith of so many people as severely as the Holocaust. Viennese psychiatrist Victor Frankl was one of the survivors of the

Nazis' atrocities. He spent 1942 to 1945 in the concentration camps of Auschwitz and Dachau. Frankl once said, "A weak faith is weakened by predicaments and catastrophes whereas a strong faith is strengthened by them." Despite the horrors he witnessed and the treatment he suffered, his faith didn't weaken—it deepened.

MANAGING THE DISCIPLINE OF FAITH

Thousands of books have been written on how to live out the discipline of faith. Perhaps that is so because it is such a difficult thing to do. For me, the discipline can be captured in one simple phrase: *every day to live and lead like Jesus.* While the words are simple, following through is not. Living out the discipline of faith is the greatest challenge of my Daily Dozen. The problem is that instead of being like Jesus, I often want to be like John Maxwell. I fall short of the mark. But with God as my helper, I keep growing. And when I do follow in his footsteps and live his principles, people are helped and I am fulfilled.

Following are four suggestions for managing your discipline of faith:

1. Embrace the Value of Faith

I've already given a number of reasons why I think faith is beneficial. But let me add to that list. There are some things in life you will arrive at only through faith. In the past, many people hoped that science would provide all the answers to life's questions. But science cannot do that.

Ironically, what is embraced as scientific fact changes from generation to generation. Just look at the way scientists have viewed our solar system. Ptolemy believed the earth was at its center. Copernicus asserted that the sun was at its center and the planets moved in circular orbits around it. Kepler proved that the orbits were elliptical. Today, scientists no longer argue the structure of the solar system, but ideas about how it was formed change continually. In fact, just this week scientists found what they are calling the oldest known planet in the globular star cluster M4. They say it is a "'stunning revelation' that will force scientists to revise their ideas of planetary formation."[26]

Contrast science with faith. The core beliefs of Judaism and Christianity have not changed in thousands of years. There is a spiritual aspect to human life that cannot be denied. Spiritual needs must be met spiritually. Nothing else will fill the void.

2. Put God in the Picture

There's a story of a man driving a convertible on a mountain road who took an unexpected turn too quickly and went right over the edge. As his car fell, he managed to grab on to a tree sprouting from the cliff face as his car dropped a thousand feet to the canyon floor.

"Help!" he screamed. "Can anyone hear me?" An echo was the only response.

"God, can you hear me?" he cried.

Suddenly the clouds rolled together and a voice like thunder said, "Yes, I can hear you."

"Will you help me?"

"Yes, I will help you. Do you believe in me?"

"Yes, I believe in you."

"Do you trust me?"

"Yes, yes, I trust you. Please, hurry."

"If you trust me, then let go of the tree," thundered the voice.

After a long silence, the man cried, "Can anyone else hear me?"

If you want to embrace faith, you must let God into your life. No one else is worthy of our absolute and unconditional trust. Theologian F. B. Meyer said, "Unbelief puts our circumstances between us and God. Faith puts God between us and our circumstances." Who wouldn't like to have the Creator of the universe helping them? James, one of the fathers of the first-century church, advised, "Come near to God and he will come near to you."[27]

3. Associate with People of Faith

Comedian Bob Hope once went to the airport to meet his wife, Dolores, who had been doing some charity work for the Catholic Church. When her private plane pulled in, the first two people to step off the plane were Catholic priests. Then came Dolores, followed by four more Catholic priests. Hope turned to a friend near him and quipped, "I don't know why she just doesn't buy insurance like everybody else!"

It's a fact that you become more like the people you spend time with. If you desire to increase your faith, spend time with others who exercise theirs. Learn from them. Find out how they think.

4. Explore and Deepen Your Faith

Developing your faith is very similar to developing yourself physically. Perhaps that's why the Bible contains so many athletic metaphors for spiritual growth. If you want to get into good physical condition, you need to exercise your body regularly. If you don't, you not only don't gain strength and conditioning, you begin to lose what you once had.

D. L. Moody, a nineteenth-century lay preacher who founded Northfield Seminary and the Moody Bible Institute, explained how his faith developed. He said, "I prayed for faith, and thought that some day faith would come down and strike me like lightning. But faith did not seem to come. One day I read in the tenth chapter of Romans, 'Faith comes by hearing, and hearing by the word of God.' I had closed my Bible and prayed for faith. I now opened my Bible and began to study, and faith has been growing ever since."

Your Faith Decision Today

Where do you stand when it comes to faith today? Ask yourself these three questions:

1. Have I already made the decision to deepen and live out my faith daily?
2. If so, when did I make that decision?
3. What exactly did I decide?

Your Faith Discipline Every Day

Based on the decision you made concerning faith, what is the one discipline you must practice *today and every day* in order to be successful?

9

RELATIONSHIPS

When I was in college in 1965, I took Psychology 101 with Dr. David Van Hoose. One day as he was lecturing, he said something that really got my attention. He remarked, "If you have one true friend in life, you are very fortunate. If you have two real friends, it is highly unusual." I was dumbfounded. As a sanguine student, I thought everyone had lots of friends. Even though Dr. Van Hoose defined friendships as relationships characterized by unconditional love, I was still shocked.

Relationships had always been important to me, and I developed good people skills at a young age. When I was in my early teens, my father encouraged me to read *How to Win Friends and Influence People* by Dale Carnegie. I've always remembered the advice that the master of relationships gave in the book: "In order to make friends, one must first be friendly."[28] I had embraced that recommendation, but after hearing the words of my psychology professor, I determined to be more intentional and take relationships to a new level in my life. That's when I made this relationship decision: *I will initiate and make an investment in relationships with others.*

MAKING THE DECISION TO INITIATE AND INVEST IN SOLID RELATIONSHIPS DAILY

I think a lot of people don't take responsibility for the relationships in their lives. They simply let things happen to them rather than being intentional about it. But to have the kind of solid relationships that bring fulfillment, you have to change your mind-set when it comes to dealing with others. Here are some ways you can do that:

Place a High Value on People

Let's face it, if you don't care about people, you are unlikely to make building good relationships a priority in your life. My friend Ken Blanchard, author of *Whale Done* and *Raving Fans,* jokes that the Department of Motor Vehicles evidently seeks out and hires people who hate people. When you go to get your driver's license, you expect to be treated poorly. What onetime national salesman of the year Les Giblin said is true: "You can't make the other fellow feel important in your presence if you secretly feel that he is a nobody."

The solution is to place a high value on people. Expect the best from everyone. Assume people's motives are good unless they prove them to be otherwise. Value them by their best moments. And give them your friendship rather than asking for theirs. That will ultimately be their decision.

Learn to Understand People

Tom Peters and Nancy Austin, authors of *A Passion for Excellence*, state that "the number one managerial productivity problem in America is, quite simply, managers who are out of touch with their people and out of touch with their customers."[29] I think one possible explanation is that some managers don't value people. But that isn't always true. Many people care about others, but they still remain out of touch. In those cases, I think the problem is that they don't understand people.

If you desire to improve your understanding of people so that you can build positive relationships, then keep in mind the following truths about people—and actions you can take to bridge the gap often caused by them:

- People are insecure . . . give them confidence.
- People want to feel special . . . sincerely compliment them.
- People desire a better tomorrow . . . show them hope.
- People need to be understood . . . listen to them.
- People are selfish . . . speak to their needs first.
- People get emotionally low . . . encourage them.
- People want to be associated with success . . . help them win.

When you understand people, don't take their shortcomings personally, and help them to succeed, you lay the groundwork for good relationships.

Give Respect Freely but Expect to Earn It from Others

One day a man arriving at the airport saw a well-dressed businessman yelling at a porter about the way he was handling his luggage. The more irate the businessman became, the calmer and more professional the porter appeared. When the abusive man left, the first man complimented the porter on his restraint. "Oh, it was nothing," said the porter. "You know, that man's going to Miami, but his bags— they're going to Kalamazoo." People who disrespect others always hurt themselves relationally—and they often reap other negative consequences.

I believe every human being deserves to be treated with respect because everyone has value. I also have observed that giving people respect first is one of the most effective ways of interacting with others. However, that doesn't mean you can demand respect in return. You must earn it. If you respect yourself, respect others, and exhibit competence, others will almost always give you respect. If everyone treated others with respect, the world would be a better place.

Commit Yourself to Adding Value to Others

Nineteenth-century English preacher Charles Spurgeon advised, "Carve your name on hearts and not on marble." The best way to do that is to add value to others. Do that by:

- Looking for ability in others
- Helping others discover their ability
- Helping others develop their ability

Some people approach every interaction with others as a transaction. They're willing to add value, but only if they expect to receive value in return. If you want to make relationships a priority, you must check your motives to be sure you are not trying to manipulate others for your own gain.

To make sure your motives are right, take this advice from Leo Buscaglia, who wrote *Loving Each Other*: "Always start a relationship by asking: Do I have ulterior motives for wanting to relate to this person? Is my caring conditional? Am I trying to escape something? Am I planning to change the person? Do I need this person to help me make up for a deficiency in myself? If your answer to any of these questions is 'yes,' leave the person alone. He or she is better off without you."[30]

MANAGING THE DISCIPLINE OF RELATIONSHIP BUILDING

I think a lot of the time we take relationships for granted. Because of that, we don't always give them the attention they deserve or require. But good relationships require a lot of effort. To keep me on track in my relationships so that

I'm investing in them as I must to make them successful, I practice this discipline: ***Every day I make the conscious effort to deposit goodwill into my relationships with others.***

That means I give more than I expect to receive, love others unconditionally, look for ways to add value to others, and bring joy to the relationships I hold dear. Every evening, I evaluate this area of my life by asking myself, "Have I been thoughtful toward people today? Would they express joy that they have spent time with me?" If the answer is yes, then I've done my part.

If you want to improve your relationships through your everyday actions, then do the following:

Put Others First

The best way to start off on the right foot is to put others first. The most basic way to do that is to practice the Golden Rule: Do unto others as you would have them do unto you. If you take that mind-set into all your interactions with others, you can't go wrong. But there are also other ways to show people they matter and that you are interested in their well-being: Walk slowly through the crowd, remember people's names, smile at everyone, and be quick to offer help. People don't care how much you know until they know how much you care.

Don't Carry Emotional Baggage

Few things weigh as much as old hurts and offenses carried day after day in a person's life. If you want to enjoy your time with other people, you've got to get rid of that kind of stuff. You can't keep score of old wrongs and expect to make relationships right. If someone has hurt you and you need to address it and get it out onto the table, then do it right away. Resolve it and get beyond it. If it's not worth bringing up, forget about it and move on.

Give Time to Your Most Valuable Relationships

Most people give away their relational energy on a first-come, first-served basis. Whoever gets their attention first gobbles up their time and relational energy. That's why the squeaky wheels instead of the high producers at work consume so much attention and why so many people have nothing left to give when they get home from work. Since you've already read the chapter on family, you should know that I believe your family provides the most valuable relationships in your life. They should come first as you plan to spend your time. After that should come your next most important relationships. It's a matter of practicing good priorities.

Serve Others Gladly

I once heard an airline executive explain how difficult it is to hire and train people for his industry. He said that service is the only thing they have to sell, but it is the toughest thing to teach because nobody wants to be thought of as a servant.

Helen Keller said, "Life is an exciting business and most exciting when lived for others." I think that's true. The longer I live, the more convinced I am that adding value to others is the greatest thing we can do in this life. Because of that, when I serve, I try to do so cheerfully and with the greatest impact.

Express Love and Appreciation Often

After I had my heart attack, a lot of people asked me, "What was your dominant emotion? Was it fear, panic, questions?" My answer surprised many of them. In fact, it really surprised me. It was love. More than anything else in those moments of pain when I wasn't sure whether I would live or die, I wanted to tell the people closest to me how much I loved them—my family, the people who work with me, longtime friends. I learned that you can't tell the people you love how much you love them too often.

I think many people believe the best way they can help others is to criticize them, to give them the benefit of their "wisdom." I disagree. The best way to help people is to see the best in them. I want to encourage every person I meet. I want them to know the good I see in them. I practice the 101 percent principle. I look for the one thing I admire in them and give them 100 percent encouragement for it. It helps me to like them. It helps them to like me. And what else could be better for starting a relationship?

Your Relationship Decision Today

Where do you stand when it comes to relationships today? Ask yourself these three questions:

1. Have I already made the decision to initiate and invest in solid relationships daily?
2. If so, when did I make that decision?
3. What exactly did I decide?

Your Relationship Discipline Every Day

Based on the decision you made concerning relationships, what is the one discipline you must practice *today and every day* in order to be successful?

10

GENEROSITY

When my wife, Margaret, and I started our life together in the weeks after our wedding, we moved to Hillham, Indiana, where I took my first job. The church that hired me was able to pay only eighty dollars a week, so Margaret worked several jobs to help us make ends meet. Those days were very difficult for us financially, yet they were still filled with great joy.

At that time, my brother, Larry, was tasting early success in the business world and was doing very well financially. Larry and his wife, Anita, saw that we were struggling, and for those first few years, they were very generous to us. The only vacations we had were ones they invited us on and paid for. All my good clothes were the result of their generosity. Larry paid my expenses as I worked on a business degree. We will always be grateful to them.

As I look back on those days, three thoughts are clear to me. First, Margaret and I were never jealous of Larry and

Anita's financial success. We were thrilled for them, and not once did we covet what they had. Second, we could see that their generous spirit was a tremendous source of joy for them and a blessing for us. Third, I began to realize the incredible value of having a generous lifestyle toward others. That's when I made another of my life decisions: *I will live to give.* Margaret and I recognized that greatness is not defined by what a person receives, but by what that person gives. True generosity isn't a function of income—it begins with the heart. It's about serving others and looking for ways to add value to them. That's the way to achieve significance in your life.

MAKING THE DECISION TO PLAN FOR AND MODEL GENEROSITY DAILY

If you desire to become generous and make generosity part of your daily life, then do the following:

Give Others Your Money

The way people handle money colors their attitude about many other aspects of their lives. Wherever your money is, that's where your attention goes. Haven't you found that to be true? If you invest heavily in the stock market, you probably check the financial page or your earning statements frequently. If you spend a large amount of money on a house, you probably spend a lot of time and effort taking care of it. If you give a lot of money to a church or favorite charity, you care how the money is used and whether the organization succeeds.

That truth is even borne out in the Scriptures. In fact, there are a lot of insights about money contained in the Bible. Believe it or not, the Bible has more teachings about money than about prayer! One of the most telling observations is this one: "Where your treasure is, there your heart will be also."[31]

If you give money to people, either directly or through a worthy charity, you will care about people more. And that will help to foster a more generous spirit in you. You have to "prime the pump," so to speak, and then the giving will flow. If you wait until you *feel* like it to give, you may wait forever. You become generous by first giving money away. Andrew Carnegie, the steel magnate who gave away millions of dollars, said, "No man becomes rich unless he enriches others."

Give Others Yourself

What do people often value more than your money? The answer is your time and attention. Think about it. What takes greater effort: writing a check or giving your time? What shows the greater level of commitment? My friend Larry Burkett said, "Where there is no giving, there is no commitment." I believe that is true. The people closest to you would rather have you than your money. Nothing can take the place of a spouse's affection. A child desires to have a parent's undivided attention more than anything else. Even sharp employees with great potential understand that a good mentor is more valuable than a mere monetary reward. Money may buy stuff, but a good mentor buys a better future. When you give the gift of yourself, you are being as generous as you can be.

Take a moment to recall the people who've had the greatest impact in your life. Perhaps you had a teacher who helped you understand that you could think and learn. Maybe you had a parent, aunt, or uncle who made you feel loved and accepted. Or perhaps a coach or employer saw your potential, painted a positive picture of your future, and then challenged and equipped you to reach for something better. They helped you to become the person you were always meant to be. What gift could be greater than that?

Rabbi Harold Kushner said, "The purpose of life is not to win. The purpose of life is to grow and to share. When you come to look back on all that you have done in life, you will get more satisfaction from the pleasure you brought to other people's lives than you will from the times that you outdid and defeated them." When you invest in another person just for the sake of seeing that person blossom, with no thought to any benefit you might receive, you will be the kind of generous person others want to be around. And your days truly will be masterpieces.

Some people see giving to others as more than just a kind and beneficial act. They see it as an obligation. Physician and missionary Sir Wilfred T. Grenfell said, "The service we render to others is really the rent we pay for our room on this earth. It is obvious that man is himself a traveler; that the purpose of this world is not 'to have and to hold' but 'to give and to serve.' There can be no other meaning."

MANAGING THE DISCIPLINE OF GENEROSITY

It's very easy to live only for yourself. In fact, that may be every person's natural bent. I know it's mine. But we can take another path—to be generous. My desire is to be the kind of person I would like to be around. To help with that, I practice this discipline, reminding myself: ***Every day I will add value to others.***

What does it mean to add value to others? How do you do it? Here is how to start:

- **Value people:** This means treating everyone with respect.
- **Know what people value:** This means listening and seeking to understand others.
- **Make myself more valuable:** This means growing in order to give, because I cannot give what I do not possess.
- **Do things that God values:** Since he unconditionally loves people, so must I.

When you value people, you open the door to generosity. And it becomes much easier to plan for and model generosity daily. If you've adopted that mind-set, you're ready to be generous to others. Think about these things as you strive to practice the discipline of generosity every day:

Don't Wait for Prosperity to Become Generous

Because I spent over twenty-five years in the ministry, I know a lot about people's giving patterns and their attitudes about money. One of the things I've heard many people say is that if they ever have a lot of money, *then* they will become generous. People who say such things are usually fooling themselves.

A person's level of income and desire to give have nothing to do with each other. Some of the most generous people I know have nothing materially. And I know plenty of people who have a lot to give but no heart to give it. Statistics bear that out. The average personal income in the state of Mississippi is the second lowest in the United States ranked by state, yet the state is ranked sixth in charitable giving. In contrast, New Hampshire is ranked sixth in average personal income. Do you know where they rank in charitable giving as a percentage of income? They're forty-fifth.[32]

Prosperity and high income don't help people become generous. In fact, Henry Ward Beecher, the brother of novelist Harriet Beecher Stowe, warned that they could actually make people less likely to give. He said, "Watch lest prosperity destroy generosity." People in the United States live in the most prosperous country in the world during the most prosperous time in its history. Yet they still don't give much. Today, 2.5 percent of our income goes to charitable giving. That's lower than it was during the Great Depression (2.9 percent).[33] And 80 percent of Americans who earn at least $1 million a year leave nothing to charity in their wills.[34]

People give not from the top of their purses, but from the bottom of their hearts. If you desire to become a more generous person, don't wait for your income to change. Change your heart. Do that, and you can become a giver regardless of your income or circumstances.

Find a Reason to Give Every Day

It may be easy for people to find reasons *not* to give. But it's just as easy to find good reasons *to* give. You just need to look for them. Go out of your way to find reasons *to* give. Look for a compelling cause. Find an urgent need. Look for a group that is making an impact. Seek out leaders you know and believe in. Give to organizations you respect and trust. They're all around you; you just need to make it a priority.

Find People to Receive Every Day

D. L. Moody, founder of the Moody Bible Institute, said, "Do all the good you can, to all the people you can, in all the ways you can, as long as you can." When it comes right down to it, the recipients of your generosity are never causes, institutions, or organizations. Ultimately, the recipients are individual people.

People in need of help are all around you. You don't need to go halfway around the world or send a check overseas to help and serve others, although there's nothing wrong with doing those things. But there are plenty of people closer to home who can benefit from what you have to offer—people in your own town, your own neighborhood, even your own home. Being generous means keeping your eyes open for opportunities to give to everyone, whether it's through mentoring a colleague, feeding a homeless person, sharing your faith with a friend, or spending time with your kids. Civil rights leader Martin Luther King, Jr., said, "Life's most persistent and urgent question is, 'What are we doing for others?' " How you answer that question is a measure of your generosity. And the more generous you are, the greater your opportunity to do something significant for others.

Your Generosity Decision Today

Where do you stand when it comes to generosity today? Ask yourself these three questions:

1. Have I already made the decision to plan for and model generosity daily?
2. If so, when did I make that decision?
3. What exactly did I decide?

Your Generosity Discipline Every Day

Based on the decision you made concerning generosity, what is the one discipline you must practice *today and every day* in order to be successful?

11

VALUES

I grew up in a home where great values were taught and lived out, but I didn't make a conscious decision to embrace good values and live them out until 1970 when I was twenty-three years old. That year I read *Spiritual Leadership* by J. Oswald Sanders.[35] It changed my life. Up until then, I had been a people pleaser and census taker in my leadership. I led people according to what was popular. Ninety percent of the time that was okay. But on the occasions when a real leadership decision was required, when I really needed to do something that would be unpopular, I wavered. Reading Sanders's book made me realize that I was not leading according to my values, and it gave me the courage to do the right thing, even if it wasn't popular. I made the decision: *I will lead others based on the values I embrace.*

I still have my copy of *Spiritual Leadership* because it marked me. Inside the back cover, I wrote three commitments that would shape the rest of my life. The book challenged me:

1. **To be God's man:** No matter where my work takes me, I desire to be in the center of God's will.
2. **To develop my potential to the best of my ability:** I will never allow myself to be lazy, indifferent, or noncommittal concerning spiritually lost people.
3. **To be a true spiritual leader:** God is my idol, Jesus is my pattern, and the Bible provides my direction. Too many men are stereotyped leaders. Their whole outlook is warped by their surroundings. I will not, with God's help, be poured into another man's mold or teach what I do not believe.

For thirty-four years, I've continually asked myself this question: "Am I leading others according to the values I embrace?" At times, my value-based leadership has alienated me from others, but never from myself.

MAKING THE DECISION TO EMBRACE AND PRACTICE GOOD VALUES DAILY

Comedian Fred Allen said, "You only live once. But if you work it right, once is enough." How can people work it right? By knowing their values and living by them every day. Do that, and you will have few regrets at the end of your life. Here are some suggestions to help you get started:

Create a List of Good Values

Begin writing down any and every idea you have concerning values. List every admirable character quality you can think of. As an aspect of your life comes to mind, try to capture what's important to you about it. Ultimately, your values should not be determined by externals, such as your profession or your environment, but as you consider such things, you will be prompted to be thorough in your thinking.

When you think you've exhausted every possible idea, set the list aside for a while but keep thinking about it in the back of your mind. When new ideas come, add them to the list. You may also want to do some reading to stir your thinking and see if you've missed anything.

After a few weeks, begin to combine ideas on the list. (For example, "truthfulness" and "integrity" really overlap. So do "commitment" and "hard work." Choose one—or pick another word that better describes both terms together.) Then narrow it down. You can't possibly live out twenty or fifty values, so you need to start eliminating some. Which are based on truth and your highest ideals? Which items on your list truly represent the core of your being? Which will be lasting? What would you be willing to live for? To die for? Start eliminating anything that's superficial or temporary. If you're married, involve your spouse in this process. Your lists of values may not be identical, but they should have much in common. And if any of your values seem to be at odds with your spouse's, beware. You need to talk these values through and find out where you really stand, or there will always be conflict in your marriage.

Embrace Those Good Values

Years ago my friend Jim Dobson, the founder of Focus on the Family, delivered the commencement address at Seattle Pacific University. In it he spoke about the midlife crisis that many people experience between the ages of thirty-five and fifty. He said, "I believe that it is more a phenomenon of a wrong value system than it is the age group in which it occurs. All of a sudden you realize that the ladder you've been climbing is leaning against the wrong wall." Clarifying and embracing your values can help you to prevent such a thing from happening to you.

Make a Decision to Live Those Values Daily

True life change begins when you decide to change your value system, because it's foundational to everything you do. My friend Pat Williams, senior vice president of the Orlando Magic, once told me that when Roy Disney was asked about the secret of Disney's success, he used to say that the company was managed by values, which led to ease in good decision making. The same is true for an individual.

Physicist Albert Einstein advised, "Try not to become men of success. Rather, become men of value." Why would he say such a thing? Because he knew that having values keeps a person focused on the important things. That leads to a better quality of life, a life of integrity. Besides, if you focus on your values, success is likely to follow anyway.

MANAGING THE DISCIPLINE OF VALUES

Managing your life according to your values isn't easy. Why? Because your values will be tested daily by those who do not embrace them. Negative people may discount you when you display a positive attitude. People without families may not understand your devotion to your family. Unteachable people won't understand your dedication to personal growth. And those whose priorities are different from yours will try to convince you to follow them or make unwise compromises.

The discipline I practice to battle this is simple: ***Every day I review and reflect on my values***. To help me do that, I keep a list of my Daily Dozen in my "thinking companion," a little notebook I always keep with me so that I can write down ideas and jot down reminders of things to tell Margaret. Every time I open the notebook, I see those twelve values. I also give myself the twelve-minute test. At the end of each day, I spend one minute reviewing and reflecting on each of the Daily Dozen. That way, I stay on track and am less likely to drift away from living out my values.

To become better at embracing and practicing your values every day, follow these guidelines:

Articulate and Embrace Your Values Daily

How do you manage something as abstract as your values? You begin by putting them in concrete form. Once you've created your list of values, write a descriptive statement for each one explaining how you intend to apply it to your life and what benefit or direction that will bring.

Keep that document where you can see it every day. Think about your values often to help them "soak in." As you go through your day and face decisions, measure your choices against your values. And whenever it's appropriate, talk about them. It not only cements your values in your mind and helps you to practice them, but it also adds a level of accountability.

Good business leaders understand the importance of speaking about their values continually. Stew Leonard, president of the grocery store chain Stew Leonard's, says that he continually verbalizes the value of the company's customers. "We don't see customers the way you do," he says. "Our people imagine each of our customers with $50,000 tattooed on their forehead." How is that? It's simply a matter of math:

$100	Average amount each customer spends per week
x 50	Number of weeks per year customers shop his store
x 10	Average number of years residents live in his city
= $50,000	The value of each customer[36]

When you embrace your values wholeheartedly and articulate them continually, you dramatically increase your chances of living them.

Compare Your Values to Your Practices Daily

The gap between knowing and doing is significantly greater than the gap between ignorance and knowledge. A person who identifies and articulates his values but doesn't practice them is like a salesman who makes promises to a customer and then fails to deliver. He has no credibility. In business, the result is that the person loses his job. In life, the person loses his integrity.

In 1995, Girish Shah, an assistant controller for a division of a Fortune 500 company, was charged with embezzling $988,000 from the company over an eight-year period. He pleaded no contest in court, and he was prepared to repay $728,000 immediately and borrow additional money from relatives to repay the rest.

The CEO of the company was outraged. To court officials he wrote:

> I view Mr. Shah's crime as particularly egregious. Not only did he steal from the stockholders of this Fortune 500 company, but he breached the fiduciary duty placed in him by the company and his supervisors. . . . I urge you to impress upon Mr. Shah and those others who commit similar crimes that wrongdoing of this nature against society is considered a grave matter by the Texas Court and will not be condoned.[37]

You know what was ironic about that statement? It was made by Tyco CEO Dennis Kozlowski, the man later charged with looting $600 million from that same company with the help of two other executives.[38] Evidently this disconnection between his stated values and his practices was a pattern. Kozlowski used to brag to people about how frugal he was with the company's money. He often pointed out the spartan offices the company possessed in one location even as he maintained lavishly appointed offices in another.

Discrepancies between values and practices create chaos in a person's life. If you talk your values but neglect to walk them, then you will continually undermine your integrity and credibility. And that will happen even if you are unaware of your behavior and are not doing it intentionally.

Live Out Your Values Regardless of Your Feelings

Many people get into trouble when their values and their feelings collide. When you're feeling good and everything's going your way, it's not difficult to consistently live out your values. However, when your values determine you should take an action that will hurt you or cost you something, it can be harder to follow through.

If one of your values is integrity and you found a bank bag of money on the street that you suspected was stolen, you probably wouldn't have too difficult a time turning the money in to the police. But what if you saw your boss stealing from the company you work for and you knew that calling attention to it would get you fired? That choice would be more difficult, especially if you knew that losing your job might cost you your house or ruin you financially.

Successful people do what's right no matter how they

feel about it. They don't expect to be able to feel their way into acting. They act first and then hope that their feelings follow suit. Usually that doesn't involve anything dramatic. The tough decisions are the everyday ones. For example, if good health is one of my values, will I exercise even though I don't feel like it in the morning? Will I refrain from eating a big piece of chocolate cake even though I really want it? For me to be successful, my values—not my feelings— need to control my actions. Ken Blanchard and Norman Vincent Peale wrote in *The Power of Ethical Management*, "Nice guys may appear to finish last, but usually they are running in a different race."[39] Living by your values is running in a different race.

Evaluate Each Day in Light of Your Values

Most people take very little time to do any reflective thinking, yet that is necessary for anyone who wants to live out his values with consistency. Ben Franklin used to get up in the morning asking himself, "What good will I do today?" When he went to bed, he asked himself, "What good did I do today?" He was evaluating himself in light of one of his values. For the last several years, I've tried to do something similar. At the end of the day, I reflect on whether I have added value to anyone's life during the day, because that is something I desire to do every day of my life.

Your Values Decision Today

Where do you stand when it comes to values today? Ask yourself these three questions:

1. Have I already made the decision to embrace and practice good values daily?
2. If so, when did I make that decision?
3. What exactly did I decide?

Your Values Discipline Every Day

Based on the decision you made concerning values, what is the one discipline you must practice *today and every day* in order to be successful?

12

GROWTH

In 1974, a critical event occurred in my life that would change it forever. I met Kurt Kampmeir of Success Motivation, Inc., for breakfast in Lancaster, Ohio. While we were eating, Kurt posed a question. "John," he asked, "what is your plan for personal growth?"

Never at a loss for words, I tried to find things in my life that might qualify for growth. I told him about the many activities I was engaged in throughout the week. And I went into a speech about how hard I worked and the gains I was making in my organization. I must have talked for ten minutes, until I finally ran out of gas. Kurt listened patiently, but then he finally smiled and said, "You don't have a personal plan for growth, do you?"

"No," I finally admitted.

"You know," Kurt said simply, "growth is not an automatic process."

And that's when it hit me. I wasn't doing anything intentional or strategic to make myself better. And in that moment, I made the decision: *I will develop and follow a personal growth plan for my life.*

That night, I went home and talked to Margaret about my conversation with Kurt and what I had learned that day. I showed her the workbook and tapes that Kurt was selling. I knew those resources could help us grow. The cost was $745, a huge sum for us at the time. We couldn't afford it—but we couldn't afford not to get it either. Up till then I had always believed in my own potential, but I had never thought about having a way to increase and reach it. We recognized that Kurt wasn't just trying to make a sale. He was offering a way for us to change our lives and achieve our dreams.

A couple of important things happened that night. First, we figured out how to scrape together the money to buy the resources. It would require us to make sacrifices in our already-tight budget for the next six months. But more important, Margaret and I made a commitment to grow together as a couple. From that day on, we learned together, we traveled together, and we sacrificed together in order to grow. It was a wise decision. While too many couples grow apart, we were growing together.

MAKING THE DECISION TO SEEK AND EXPERIENCE GROWTH DAILY

If you're ready to make the decision to pursue growth and experience improvement every day, then do the following:

Answer the Question: What Is My Potential?

I saw a story about a St. Louis doctor who met a young man in high school who had lost his hand at the wrist. When the doctor asked about his handicap, the teenager responded, "I don't have a handicap, sir. I just don't have a right hand." The doctor later learned that the young man was one of the leading scorers on his high school football team.

The greatest handicap a person has is not realizing his potential. What dreams do you have that are just waiting to be fulfilled? What gifts and talents are inside you that are dying to be drawn out and developed? The gap between your vision and your present reality can only be filled through a commitment to maximize your potential.

Make a Commitment to Change

Author William Feather said, "The only thrill worthwhile is the one that comes from making something out of yourself." To make something out of yourself, you need to be willing to change, for without change, there can be no growth. The problem most people have is that they want things to stay the same yet also get better. Obviously, that can't happen. If you truly want to grow, then commit yourself to not only accepting change, but seeking it.

Set Growth Goals

When I first began going after personal growth using Kurt Kampmeir's materials, I pursued a growth plan that was foundational rather than specific. And that was okay then. I was in my midtwenties and I was just getting started. But as I got older, more experienced, and further in my career, I started to focus my growth in a few key areas. One was communication. That made sense for me, not only because I spoke to audiences four or five times a week, but also because I had some natural ability in that area. Another area was leadership—something I needed to do well every day of my life to succeed in my career.

As you plan your growth, it will benefit you greatly to be focused. Peter Drucker, the father of modern management, said, "The great mystery isn't that people do things badly but that they occasionally do a few things well. The only thing that is universal is incompetence. Strength is always specific. Nobody ever commented, for example, that the great violinist Jascha Heifetz probably couldn't play the trumpet very well."[40] In the chapter on priorities, I encouraged you to focus your priorities in three main areas: requirement, return, and reward. You should use the same criteria for your personal growth. Focus on growing in your areas of greatest strength, not your weaknesses. And grow in areas that will add value to you personally and professionally.

Learn to Enjoy the Journey

Eugene Griessman, author of *The Path to High Achievement*, says that most grand masters of chess learn and relearn chess moves, gambits, and combinations over a period of fifteen years before they win their first world title. That's a fifth of most people's lives. If you're going to spend that much time learning something, then you had better learn to like it. If the destination appeals to you, but you cannot enjoy the journey it takes to get there, you would be wise to reexamine your priorities to make sure you have them right.

Put Yourself in a Growth Environment

I've often wondered what would have happened, when I came home to Margaret that day in 1974 after seeing Kurt Kampmeir, if she had said she didn't want to grow with me and that $745 was too much money for that personal growth kit. I wonder because I know that her companionship and partnership on the personal growth journey have made all the difference. By working together to improve ourselves, we created a growth environment that helped us to broaden our horizons and live a life that we never could have imagined when we first got married. And that environment continued as we raised our children. When Elizabeth and Joel Porter were growing up, their mental, emotional, and spiritual growth were our highest priorities.

I've been told that certain species of fish will grow according to the size of their environment. Put them in a tiny aquarium, and they remain small even at adulthood. Release them into a huge natural body of water, and they grow to their intended size. People are similar. If they live in a harsh and limiting environment, they stay small. But put them someplace that encourages growth, and they will expand to reach their potential.

MANAGING THE DISCIPLINE OF GROWTH

When I finished working through Kurt Kampmeir's materials, my appetite was whetted for more growth. And it was then that I determined to practice this discipline of growth: *Every day I will grow on purpose with my plan.* Margaret and I continued to do much of our growing together, but each of us also began tailoring our growth plans to our individual strengths and needs. One of the results of learning is that you realize how far you still need to go, and the more we learned, the hungrier we were for more growth.

As you prepare to embrace the disciplines of growth, I want to encourage you to do the following:

Make It Your Goal to Grow in Some Way Every Day

In 1972, high school swimmer John Naber watched the Olympics on television and was inspired. He was already an excellent swimmer, but he began thinking about making the leap to become an Olympic-caliber athlete. He figured he would have to lower his time by four seconds in four years. For you and me, that might not be too difficult, because we have such a long way to go.

But for someone like Naber, who was already well trained, that seemed impossible. Elite racers think in terms of improving by fractions of a second. Thinking about that fact, he suddenly figured out how to approach the task. If he planned to train ten months a year for the next four years, he would have to improve by a tenth of a second every month. It was still a great challenge, but he believed he could do it and be ready for the 1976 Olympics.

Naber had the right idea. And it worked. He came home with five medals, four of them gold. If you and I want to be successful in our growth, we must adopt a similar mind-set. If we desire to improve a little every day and plan it that way, then we can make great progress over the long haul.

Have a Time and Plan to Grow

One of my favorite personal growth quotations is from author and speaker Earl Nightingale. I came across it more than twenty years ago, and it made a profound impact on me. Nightingale said, "If a person will spend one hour a day on the same subject for five years, that person will be an expert on that subject." That quotation changed how I planned my personal growth. I started spending an hour a day, five days a week, studying leadership. Over time, that practice changed my life.

To make your growth intentional, strategic, and effective, you need to think it through and plan it well. To give you an idea, I'll share how I plan my growth:

- **I listen to audio lessons every week:** First of all, I'm always on the lookout for good teaching on tape or CD. Every week, I listen to seven audio lessons. Usually, their contents break down like this: Four are average, two are good to excellent, and only one may be outstanding. (If a lesson is bad, I hit the eject button after five minutes.) For every tape, I try to determine what the "take-away" is—the one item I can immediately apply—and do some thinking to try to capitalize on it. And I have every outstanding lesson transcribed so that I can read it, mark it up, and extract every bit of gold from it.

- **I read two books every month:** If you were to go to my office, you'd find two stacks of books on the worktable near my desk. Those are the books that are "on deck" waiting to be read. They are sorted into two groups, and I read one of each every month. The first stack is of excellent books that I expect will make a strong impact on me. During the month, I spend a lot of time with that kind of book, digesting its ideas, marking the pages, pulling out ideas, and thinking about how I can apply the concepts to my life. (I also file what I learn—I'll explain that in a moment.) The second stack contains average books I intend to speed-read. They may offer just a few concepts that I want to get at quickly but don't warrant a careful reading.

- **I set an appointment every month:** One of the things I look forward to most is listening to and learning from others. So every month, I set an appointment with someone who can help me grow. Before the meeting, I prepare a list of questions that correspond to an area in which I need to grow and in which the person has achieved success. I also do any other homework that I think may be necessary, such as reading any books the person has written, but the success of the interview is determined most by the questions I prepare. My conversations with John Wooden, which I referenced in Chapter 1, were the result of one of those appointments. It was a time of empowerment for me. Whenever I spend time with great people, I expect to learn great things from them.

As you plan your strategy for growth and set aside time for it, don't forget that the more you grow, the more specific the growth should be to your needs and strengths. And any time you discover that a book, tape, or conference doesn't possess the value you'd hoped for, move on. Don't waste your time on anything of low value.

File What You Learn

I have to admit it: I am a compulsive filer. Whenever I find something that I think will be valuable to me in the future— for learning, teaching, or writing—I file it. When I hear a great tape or CD and have it transcribed, I file quotations from it. If it's really good, I might even file the whole transcript. When I read a book, I mark every quotation I want to capture and jot down what subject to file it under. If you look in the front of every good book I've read, you'll see a list of page numbers and subjects written in it. When I'm done with the book, I give it to my assistant, who copies the material and files it for me. I've been doing this for forty years!

I want to encourage you to file quotations, stories, and ideas that you find as you learn. Not only will this habit yield a great harvest of material for your future use, it will also keep you more highly focused, force you to evaluate what you're reading, and help you to bypass the junk and go for the good stuff that will stimulate you and help you grow.

Apply What You Learn

Mike Abrashoff, author of *It's Your Ship*, says, "Up is not an easy direction. It defies gravity, both cultural and magnetic."[41] Often the most difficult part of the upward climb of growth is putting into practice what you learn. Yet that is where the true value is. The final test of any learning is always application. If what you're learning can be used in some way to help and improve you or others, then it is worth the effort.

Your Growth Decision Today

Where do you stand when it comes to growth today? Ask yourself these three questions:

1. Have I already made the decision to seek and experience improvement daily?
2. If so, when did I make that decision?
3. What exactly did I decide?

Your Growth Discipline Every Day

Based on the decision you made concerning growth, what is the one discipline you must practice *today and every day* in order to be successful?

Conclusion

You really can make today great. The key is to make the most important decisions of your life and then to manage those decisions. Anyone who does that consistently can make today a masterpiece.

I hope the idea of the Daily Dozen doesn't overwhelm you. I know that you can't tackle all of them at one time. So here is what I suggest. First, determine what twelve (or ten or fifteen) decisions are important to you. Start with my list of twelve and modify it according to your own life. Then begin working on the decisions. Every month, decide which decision you will make and how you will manage it. In a year's time, you'll be amazed by how focused your life is and how it is going in the direction you desire. By making today great, you can make your life great, because when you take care of today, tomorrow will take care of itself.

Notes

1. Alec Mackenzie, *The Time Trap* (New York: Amacom, 1997).
2. "Leading Causes of Death—2000," and "International Cardiovascular Disease Statistics," American Heart Association, Statistical Fact Sheets, www.americanheart .org (accessed July 18, 2003).
3. Bernie S. Siegel, *Peace, Love and Healing* (New York: HarperCollins, 1995).
4. "UC Berkeley Epidemiologist Wins Olympic Medal for Studies Showing Exercise Protects against Heart Disease," news release, July 1, 1994, University of California Berkeley Public Information Office, www.berkeley .edu/news (accessed December 8, 2003).
5. "Building a Better Dad," *Today's Health and Wellness*, 26.
6. "New Report Sheds Light on Trends and Patterns in Marriage, Divorce, and Cohabitation," National Center for Health Statistics, www.cdc.gov/hchs/releases/ 02news/div_mar_cobah.htm (accessed June 19, 2003).
7. "Profile for United States: Indicators of Child Well Being," Kids Count, www.aecf.org (accessed June 19, 2003).

8. Matthew Cooper, "Going to Chapel," *Time*, June 10, 2002, 31.

9. Executive Leadership Foundation, Inc., *Absolute Ethics: A Proven System of True Profitability* (Tucker, GA, 1987), 18.

10. Norman Vincent Peale, *The Power of Positive Thinking* (New York: Ballantine Books, 1996).

11. James Allen, *As a Man Thinketh* (Camarillo, CA).

12. *Leadership*, Spring 2001, 83.

13. John C. Maxwell, *Thinking for a Change: 11 Ways Highly Successful People Approach Life and Work* (New York: Warner Books, 2003).

14. Anne Lamott, *Bird by Bird: Instructions on the Writing Life* (Landover Hills, MD: Anchor, 1995).

15. *Leadership*, Spring 2001, 84.

16. Philippians 4:8 NRSV.

17. "The Fall of France," www.leesaunders.com/html/Fo France.htm (accessed August 15, 2003).

18. Winston Churchill, *The Wit and Wisdom of Winston Churchill*, edited by James C. Humes (New York: Harper Perennial, 1994), 121.

19. Henry W. Longfellow, "The Ladder of St. Augustine."

20. Warren Wiersbe, *In Praise of Plodders* (Grand Rapids: Kregel, 1991).

21. Arthur Gordon, *A Touch of Wonder* (Jove Publications, 1991).

22. Quoted in Leslie E. Royale, "Debt Free Is the Way to Be," *Black Enterprise*, October 2002, www.findarticles .com (accessed July 22, 2003).

23. Ibid.

24. Quoted in Ron Blue's seminars from *USA Today*, January 7, 1997.

25. James Surowiecki, "People of Plenty," *Fast Company*, March 2003, 32.

26. John Noble Wilford, "Oldest Planet Is Revealed, Challenging Old Theories," *New York Times*, July 11, 2003, www.nytimes.com.

27. James 4:8 NIV.

28. Dale Carnegie, *How to Win Friends and Influence People* (New York: Simon and Schuster, 1936).

29. Tom Peters and Nancy Austin, *A Passion for Excellence: The Leadership Difference* (New York: Warner Books, 1989).

30. Leo Buscaglia, *Loving Each Other: The Challenge of Human Relationships* (New York: Ballantine, 1990).

31. Matthew 6:21 NIV.

32. "Numbers," *Time*, January 13, 2003, 17.

33. "Numbers," *Time*, December 6, 2002, 21.

34. *U.S. News and World Report*, December 22, 1997.

35. J. Oswald Sanders, *Spiritual Leadership*.

36. Roger Dow, *ICSA Journal*.

37. Associated Press, "Tyco's Kozlowski Took Hard Line Against Embezzling Crimes," *Seattle Times*, January 1, 2003, www.seattletimes.com.

38. Barbara Ross, Roberty Gearty, and Corky Siemaszko, "The Great Tyco Robbery," *New York Daily News*, September 12, 2002, www.nydailynews.com.

39. Ken Blanchard and Norman Vincent Peale, *The Power*

of Ethical Management (New York: William Morrow, 1988).

40. Peter Drucker, Quotes on Focus, www.leadershipnow .com (accessed November 24, 2003).

41. Mike Abrashoff, *It's Your Ship: Management Techniques from the Best Damn Ship in the Navy* (New York: Warner Books, 2002).

ABOUT THE AUTHOR

JOHN C. MAXWELL is an internationally recognized leadership expert, speaker, and author who has sold over 13 million books. His organizations have trained more than 2 million leaders worldwide. Dr. Maxwell is the founder of EQUIP and INJOY Stewardship Services. Every year he speaks to Fortune 500 companies, international government leaders, and organizations as diverse as the United States Military Academy at West Point and the National Football League. A *New York Times*, *Wall Street Journal*, and *Business Week* best-selling author, Maxwell was named the World's Top Leadership Guru by Leadershipgurus.net. He was also one of only twenty-five authors and artists named to Amazon.com's tenth-anniversary Hall of Fame. Three of his books, *The 21 Irrefutable Laws of Leadership*, *Developing the Leader Within You*, and *The 21 Indispensable Qualities of a Leader*, have each sold over a million copies.

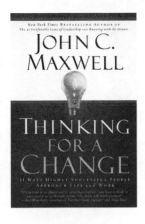

New York Times BESTSELLING AUTHOR OF
The 21 Irrefutable Laws of Leadership and Running with the Giants

JOHN C. MAXWELL

THINKING
FOR A
CHANGE

11 WAYS HIGHLY SUCCESSFUL PEOPLE
APPROACH LIFE and WORK

When your thinking is unlimited, so is your potential.

In *Thinking for a Change*, John C. Maxwell explores and identifies the specific skills you need to make your potential for success explode into results. This book won't tell you *what* to think, it tells you *how* to think. After all, success is as simple as changing your mind.

"If you want to go places you've never been before—you have to think in ways you've never thought before. This book will teach you how!"

—Ken Blanchard, coauthor of
The One Minute Manager® and *Whale Done!*

"In this important book, John Maxwell will teach you how to think in a way that will keep you ahead in these turbulent times and create exciting new opportunities and possibilities."

—Robert Kriegel, Ph.D., coauthor of
If It Ain't Broke . . . Break It!

Available now wherever books are sold.

New York Times *bestselling author and expert on leadership John C. Maxwell shares the only rule that matters—in business and in life.*

ETHICS 101

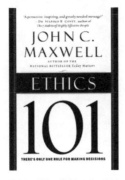

In the past few years, ethical lapses in corporate America have precipitated a need for change in business practices and business legislation. But is it always easy to see where the line is in life? What's the standard? And can it work in all situations? Maxwell thinks it can. His engaging book brilliantly demonstrates how people can live with integrity by using the Golden Rule as their standard—regardless of religion, culture, or circumstances.

"A persuasive, inspiring, and greatly needed message!"
—Dr. Stephen R. Covey, author of
The 7 Habits of Highly Effective People

Available now wherever books are sold.